LEVEL C

STECK-VAUGHN

FOCUS ON SCIENCE™

PROGRAM CONSULTANT
Elizabeth Maryott
Instructor, Mathematics-Science Division
Wayne State College
Wayne, Nebraska

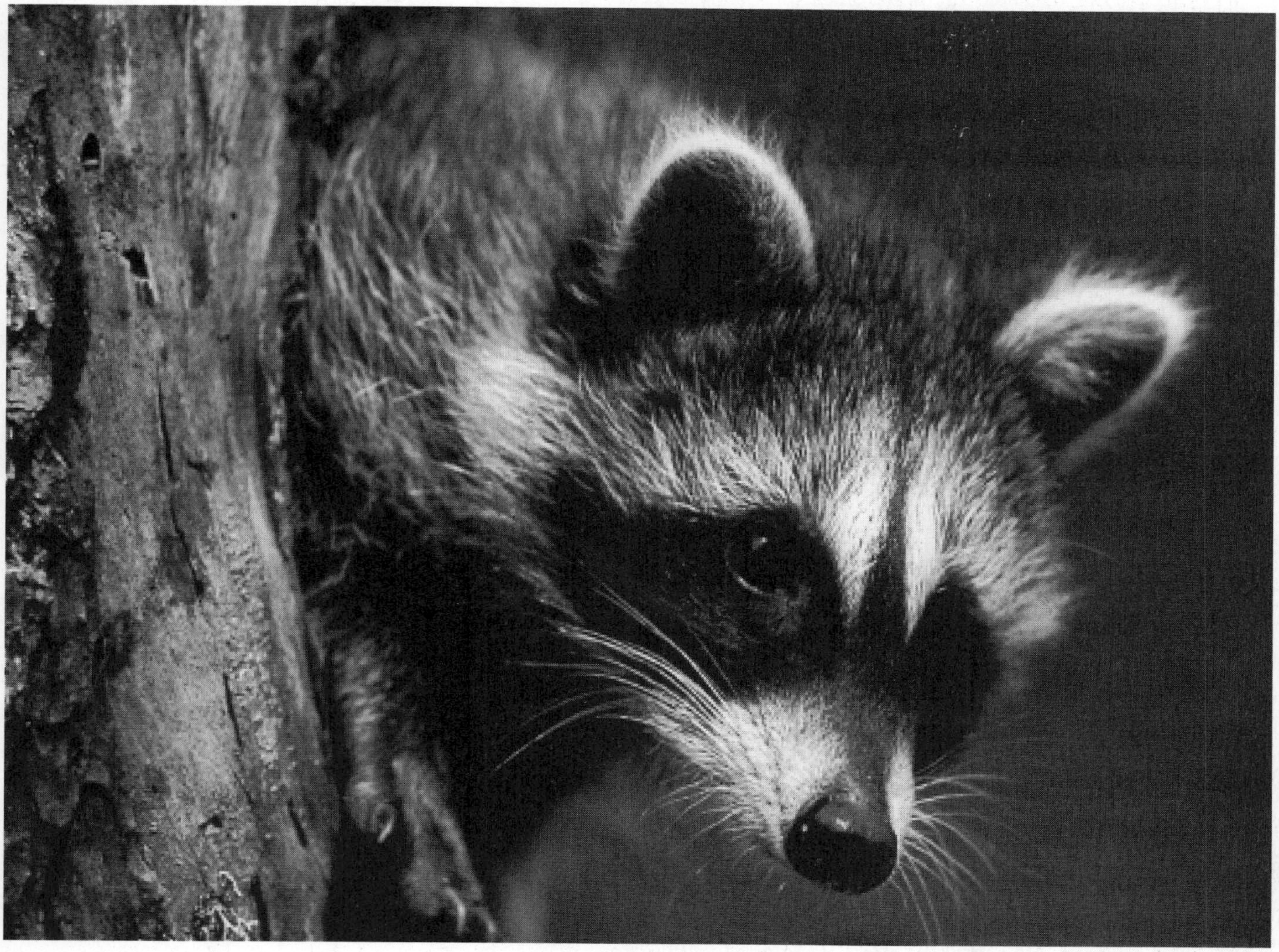

www.steck-vaughn.com

Acknowledgments

STAFF CREDITS

Executive Editor: Diane Sharpe

Project Team Leaders: Jim Cauthron, Design; Janet Jerzycki, Editorial

Editor: Linda Bullock

Design Manager: Jim Cauthron

Cover Design: Jim Cauthron

Cover Electronic Production: Alan Klemp

Program Development, Design, Illustration, and Production:
Proof Positive/Farrowlyne Associates, Inc.

PHOTOGRAPHY AND ILLUSTRATION CREDITS

Cover and Title page © Jeff Vanuga/Westlight; p. 5 Daniel Cox/Tony Stone Images; p. 6 Laurie Campbell/Tony Stone Images; p. 7 © PhotoDisk; p. 8 Tek-Nēk, Inc.; p. 8B Kathie Kelleher; p. 10A Tek-Nēk, Inc.; p. 12 Corel Photo Studio; p. 14A Tek-Nēk, Inc.; p. 14B Corel Photo Studio; p. 16A Corel Photo Studio; p. 16B Tek-Nēk. Inc.; p. 16C Tek-Nēk, Inc.; p. 18 Kathie Kelleher; p. 19 Kathie Kelleher; p. 20 Joel Snyder; p. 22 Maslowski/Visuals Unlimited; p. 23 © PhotoDisk; p. 24A Corel Photo Studio; p. 24B Tony Freeman/PhotoEdit; p. 26 Pamela Johnson; p. 28 Corel Photo Studio; p. 30 Tek-Nēk, Inc.; p. 32A Corel Photo Studio; p. 32B Tek-Nēk, Inc.; p. 33 Tek-Nēk, Inc.; p. 34 Corel Photo Studio; p. 36 Pamela Johnson; p. 38 Phil Schofield/Tony Stone Images; p. 39 © PhotoDisk; p. 40 Tek-Nēk, Inc.; p. 42 Denny Bond; p. 43 Tek-Nēk, Inc.; p. 44 Denny Bond; p. 46 Sandy McMahon; p. 48 Corel Photo Studio; p. 50 Kathie Kelleher; p. 51 Kathie Kelleher; p. 54A Mark Richards/PhotoEdit; p. 54B Stephen McBrady/PhotoEdit; p. 54C Don Mason/Stock Market; p. 55 Colin Prior/Tony Stone Images; p. 56 Galen Rowell/Tony Stone Images; p. 57 © PhotoDisk; p. 58 Tek-Nēk, Inc.; p. 60 Tek-Nēk, Inc.; p. 62 Corel Photo Studio; p. 64 Denny Bond; p. 66 Kathie Kelleher; p. 68 Kathie Kelleher; p. 70 Joel Snyder; p. 72 Mark A. Schneider/Visuals Unlimited; p. 73 © PhotoDisk; p. 74A Corel Photo Studio; p. 74B Albert Copley/Visuals Unlimited; p. 76A Steve McCutcheon/Visuals Unlimited; p. 76B Corel Photo Studio; p. 78 Kathie Kelleher; p. 80A Corel Photo Studio; p. 80B Doug Sokell/Visuals Unlimited; p. 80C Dr. E. R. Degginger/Color-Pic, Inc.; p. 80D Dan Richter/Visuals Unlimited; p. 82 Joel Snyder; p. 83 Kathie Kelleher; p. 84A Bonnie Kamin/PhotoEdit; p. 84B LINK/Visuals Unlimited; p. 86 Joel Snyder; p. 88 Ned Therrien/Visuals Unlimited; p. 89 © PhotoDisk; p. 90 Corel Photo Studio; p. 92 Tek-Nēk, Inc.; p. 94 Tek-Nēk, Inc.; p. 96 Tek-Nēk, Inc.; p. 97 Tek-Nēk, Inc.; p. 98 Kathie Kelleher; p. 100 Corel Photo Studio; p. 102 Kathie Kelleher; p. 104A Corel Photo Studio; p. 104B © Wayne E. Newton/PhotoEdit; p. 104C © Stephen Trimble; p. 105 J Nourok/PhotoEdit; p. 106 Larry Goldstein/Tony Stone Images; p. 107 © PhotoDisk; p. 108 Corel Photo Studio; p. 110 Corel Photo Studio; p. 112A Tek-Nēk, Inc.; p. 112B Stephen McBrady/PhotoEdit; p. 114 Jeff Greenberg/PhotoEdit; p. 116 Corel Photo Studio; p. 118A Tek-Nēk, Inc.; p. 118B Paul Fuqua; p. 120A and B Kathie Kelleher; p. 120C Corel Photo Studio; p. 122A Michael Newman/PhotoEdit; p. 122B Felicia Martinez/PhotoEdit; p. 122C Zigy Kaluzny/Tony Stone Images

ISBN: 0-8172-8029-4

3 4 5 6 7 8 9 DBH 04 03 02 01 00

Contents

Unit 1

Life Science

Just like you, these bear cubs have grown a lot. At one time, they were too small to see! The cubs are still growing. In time, they will be as big as their mother. Then, they will be able to have babies of their own. In this unit you will learn how living things grow and change during their lives. You will also learn how to keep healthy as your own body grows and changes.

CHAPTER

1

The Life of Plants

As you might have guessed, this plant is a young tree. It began its life as a small seed. If it gets enough of the things it needs, it will grow into a tall, strong tree. When it is big enough, the tree will make seeds. In this chapter you will learn how plants change during their lives, how they make seeds, and what seeds and young plants need to live.

What is it?

- **Every plant has one.**
- **It has four parts.**
- **It can begin all over again.**

LESSON 1 What Is a Life Cycle?

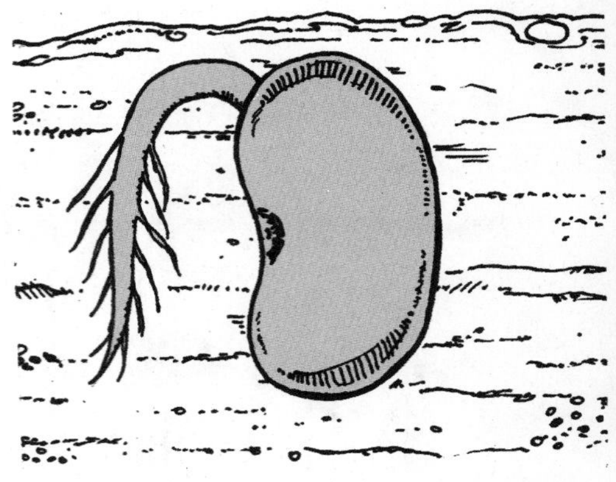

Many plants grow from seeds.

Every living thing changes during its life. The largest tree starts life as a tiny seed that you could hold in your hand. Every living thing has a **life cycle**. A life cycle is how a living thing changes during its life.

Most plants begin their life cycles as **seeds**. This is the first part of their life cycles. An **acorn** has the seed of an oak tree inside it. When the plant grows from the seed, the plant is born. Growing is the second part of a life cycle. When plants are able to make new seeds, they are **adults**. This is the third part of a life cycle. An oak tree will live for many years as an adult tree.

Oak trees grow from acorns.

All living things grow older once they become adults. Oak trees can live for many years. But someday the oak tree will grow old and begin to die. Before it dies, though, the tree will make many acorns. Some of these acorns will grow into new oak trees. Other plants, such as corn, have much shorter lives. Corn plants live for less than one year. They grow, become adults, and make new seeds during their short lives.

Like the oak tree, living things can make new living things before they die. In this way, life cycles never stop. One living thing may die and end its life cycle. But a new living thing is born and begins a new life cycle.

A. Write the word or words that best complete each sentence.

adult **grows** **life cycle** **seed**

1. Every living thing has a ________________________.
2. An acorn has the ________________________ of an oak tree inside it.
3. The second part of a plant's life cycle is when it ________________________ out of a seed.
4. A plant that can make seeds is an ________________________.

B. The sentences below tell about the life cycle of an oak tree. Write 1, 2, 3, and 4 to show the correct order.

________ The acorn has a seed inside it.

________ The plant grows old and dies.

________ The plant can make new acorns.

________ A plant grows out of the acorn.

C. Write one or more sentences to answer the question.

Daisies are plants that live for less than one year. What must a daisy do during its life to keep the life cycle going?

____

____

____

____

____

LESSON

2 What Is a Flower?

Many people grow plants that have flowers. Roses, tulips, and violets are three kinds of plants that people grow. People grow special plants to make their homes and yards pretty. But plants don't grow flowers just to be pretty. Flowers are an important part of a plant's life cycle. Flowers have special female and male parts that work together to make new plants.

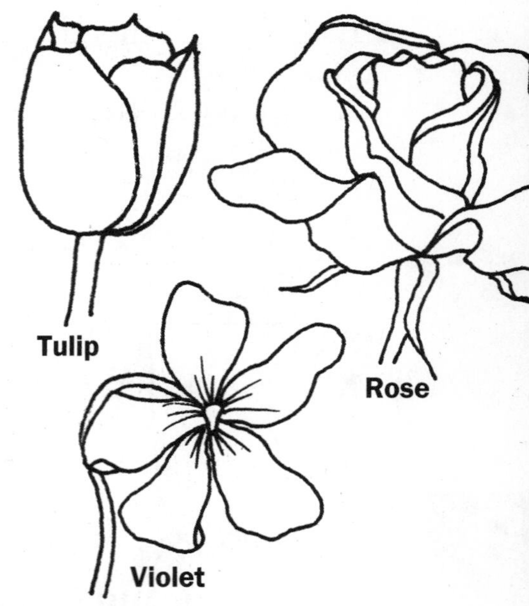

The female part of a flower is called the **pistil**. The pistil has a round bottom and a thin, sticky top. It looks like a bottle with a long neck. The bottom of the pistil is usually in the middle of the flower. The pistil has one or more tiny eggs inside it.

Parts of a Flower

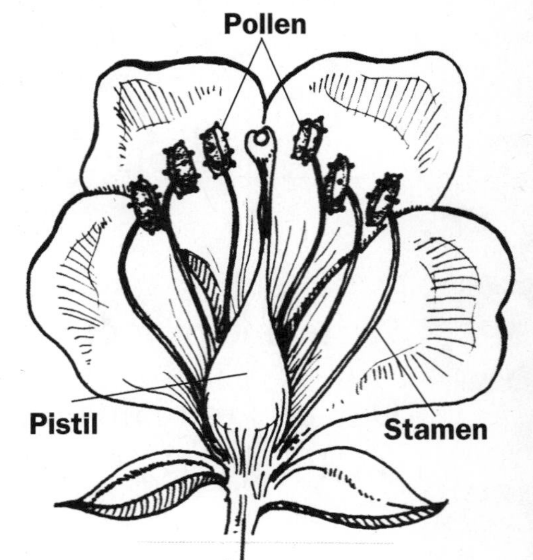

The male part of a flower is called the **stamen**. One flower can have many stamens. The stamen is long and thin with a fuzzy top. The fuzzy top of the stamen is covered with **pollen**. Pollen is made up of tiny pieces that look like colored dust.

Before the flower can make a new plant, pollen needs to move off a stamen and stick to the top of a pistil. This is called **pollination**. After pollination happens, a tiny tube grows from the pollen down into the round bottom of the pistil. The pollen travels down the tube. The pollen joins with an egg to form a seed. The seed is the beginning of a new life cycle.

A. Write the missing word or words in each sentence.

1. Flowers are an important part of a plant's

   ______________________ .

   (life cycle, seeds)

2. The pistil is the ______________________ part of a flower.
   (male, female)

3. The pistil has one or more ______________________ inside it.
   (eggs, leaves)

4. The stamen is the ______________________ part of a flower.
   (male, female)

5. The top of a stamen is covered with ______________________ .
   (pollen, eggs)

6. After pollen joins with an egg, a ______________________ forms
   inside the pistil.
   (stamen, seed)

B. Draw a line from each flower part to the words that describe it.

1. pistil	tiny pieces that look like colored dust
2. stamen	round bottom and a thin, sticky top
3. pollen	long and thin with a fuzzy top

C. Write one or more sentences to answer the questions.

Some kinds of flowers have stamens but no pistil. Do you think these flowers are male or female? Why?

____

____

____

LESSON 3

How Does Pollen Move?

There are two main kinds of pollination. One kind happens when pollen from a stamen sticks to the pistil of the same plant.

The other kind of pollination takes place when pollen from one plant travels to the pistil of another plant. Most plants use this kind of pollination. Plants need help for this kind of pollination. Plants can't move. So, they need another way to move pollen from one plant to another plant.

Butterflies help plants. They spread pollen from flower to flower. Other animals that spread pollen are bees, birds, and bats.

The wind helps move pollen between plants. The pollen of some plants is very light. Wind blows it from the flowers on one plant to the flowers on another plant. The wind can move pollen a long way before the pollen hits the sticky top of a pistil.

Animals also help move pollen between plants. Many flowers are colorful and smell good to some animals. These flowers also make a sweet juice called **nectar**. Sometimes an animal, such as a bee, sees or smells a flower. Then, it lands on the flower to get nectar. As the bee drinks the nectar, the stamens brush pollen onto its body. Then, the bee flies to another flower that has a pistil. The pollen on the bee's body brushes onto the sticky top of the flower's pistil.

The plants help feed the animal. In return, the animal helps the plants by moving pollen from flower to flower.

A. Write the missing word in each sentence.

1. One kind of pollination takes place when ______________________ from a plant sticks to the pistil of the same plant.
(stamen, pollen, wind)

2. Another kind of pollination takes place when pollen from one plant lands on the ______________________ of another plant.
(pollen, wind, pistil)

3. Some pollen moves from one plant to another on the ______________________.
(wind, pistil, sunlight)

4. Many animals spread pollen from one ______________________ to another.
(nectar, flower, egg)

B. Use each word to write a sentence about a flower.

1. bees ____

2. pollen ____

3. nectar ____

C. Write one or more sentences to answer the question.

Some plants have flowers that open at night and close during the day. What might this tell you about an animal that eats nectar from these flowers?

____

____

LESSON 4 What Is a Seed?

Many plants begin their life cycles as a seed. As you have learned, a huge oak tree starts life as a tiny acorn. Peanuts, peach pits, and grains of wheat are all seeds. This means that peanut plants, peach trees, and wheat all grow from seeds.

A seed first begins to form when pollen joins with an egg in the flower's pistil. The seed has a tiny plant inside it. It also has the food that the tiny plant will use when it starts to grow.

To keep the seed safe, the pistil grows thick around the seed and turns into a fruit. Sometimes the fruit is one that people can eat, like a peach or a cucumber. But, the winged seed of a maple tree is also a kind of fruit. All fruits keep seeds safe from harm. A seed can stay inside its fruit for a long time.

After a seed leaves its fruit, everything needs to be just right before the tiny plant can begin to grow. If it is too cold or too dry, the plant won't be able to start growing. When the seed finally becomes wet enough and warm enough, a tiny plant will begin to grow.

The best place for most seeds to grow is in warm, wet soil. First, the seed splits and the main root grows down into the ground. Then, the stem breaks up through the ground into the air. The plant has begun its life.

Seeds Inside Fruit

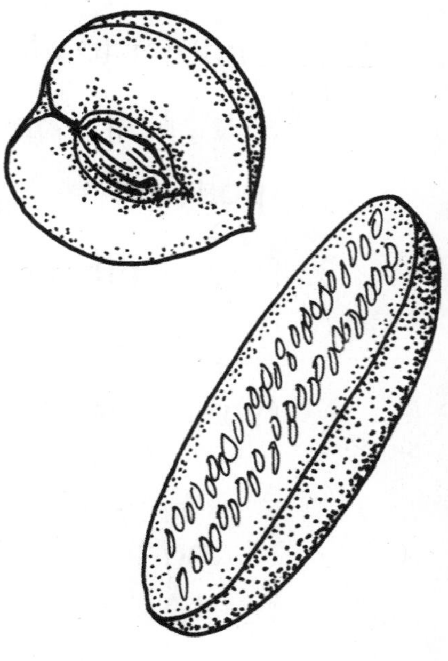

When everything is just right, a tiny plant begins to grow from the seed.

Maple Tree Seed

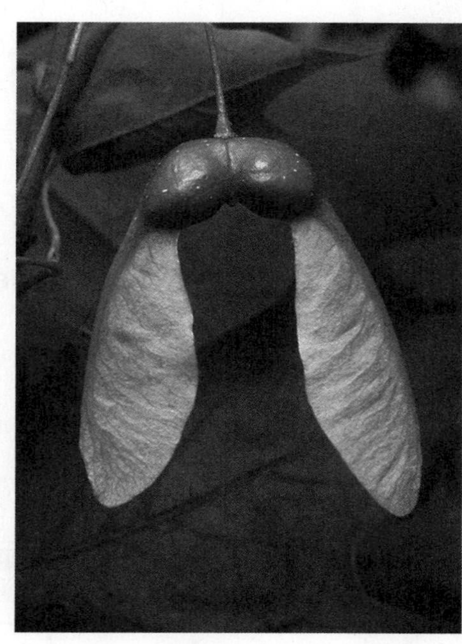

The seed of this fruit will grow into a maple tree.

A.

The sentences below tell how a new plant begins to grow. Write 1, 2, 3, 4, and 5 to show the correct order. The first one is done for you.

________ The peach is eaten and the peach pit falls to the ground.

________ The pistil of the peach tree flower grows bigger and turns into a peach.

________ A seed begins to form inside the peach tree flower.

___1___ A bee carries pollen from the stamen of one peach tree flower to the pistil of another peach tree flower.

________ The peach seed is in warm, wet soil and begins to grow.

B.

Write True if the sentence is true. Write False if the sentence is false.

________ **1.** Seeds store food for the new plant.

________ **2.** Fruit keeps the seeds safe.

________ **3.** A seed needs only sunlight to grow.

________ **4.** The root grows up through the ground.

C.

Write S after each word or words that name a seed.

1. peanut ________

2. stamen ________

3. peach pit ________

4. pollen ________

5. grain of wheat ________

D.

Write one or more sentences to answer the question.

Why do you think a seed needs to be kept safe by fruit?

____

____

How Do Seeds Travel?

Once a seed has started to grow, the new plant needs sunlight and water to stay healthy. An adult plant, like a huge oak tree, uses a lot of sunlight and water to stay alive. Under a grownup oak tree, the ground is shady. Acorns may fall from the tree to the shady ground. If a new oak tree tried to grow under the adult tree, it might not get enough sunlight or water to stay alive. This is why many seeds need to travel far away from their parent plants.

The wind carries seeds that are small and light.

Seeds travel in different ways. The wind can blow maple seeds far away from the parent maple tree. Wind can also scatter dandelion seeds across a huge field.

Animals also help seeds travel. A raccoon might pick up an apple from under an apple tree and eat it near a stream. After the raccoon eats the apple, the apple seeds might fall into the water. They might be carried down the stream. Later, they might wash up on land. There they might grow into new apple trees.

Some plants make seeds that stick to the fur of animals like dogs and sheep.

Sometimes plants make prickly seeds that stick to an animal's fur. When a sheep brushes a plant called a **thistle**, hundreds of thistle seeds stick to the sheep's coat. The seeds might stay there for days, traveling where the sheep travels. Some seeds fall off in places with good soil and enough sunlight and water. These seeds will grow into new thistle plants.

A.

Write <u>Yes</u> if the word describes something a new plant needs to stay healthy. Write <u>No</u> if the word does not describe something a new plant needs to stay healthy.

_______ **1.** apples

_______ **2.** water

_______ **3.** fur

_______ **4.** thistle

_______ **5.** sunlight

B.

Write the letter for the missing word in each sentence.

A. eats

B. fur

C. thistle

D. wind

1. A dog can carry seeds on its _______ .

2. Seeds that are small and light can travel on the _______ .

3. Seeds inside fruits can travel when an animal _______ the fruit.

4. The seeds of a _______ plant can stick to a sheep's coat.

C.

Write one or more sentences to answer the question.

One plant may make hundreds of seeds. Why does it need to make so many seeds?

___

___

___

LESSON 6 What Helps New Plants Live?

All orange trees have some things in common. They all have white flowers, dark green leaves, the same type of bark, and orange fruit. These are things that make an orange tree an orange tree. All tulips are a lot alike, and so are all violets.

But, not all orange trees, tulips, or violets are exactly alike. They are not even exactly like their parents. Some orange trees might have oranges that are bigger and sweeter than the oranges of their parents. Other orange trees might have oranges that are smaller and less sweet than the oranges of their parents. Some oak trees might be tall and strong. Other oak trees might not be as tall or as strong. Sometimes, these little differences can make a big difference in the health and life of a plant.

These two pine trees grew from seeds that fell off the same parent tree. The pine tree on the left grew faster and blocked out the light of the pine tree on the right.

For example, two pine seeds fall from the same pine tree. They begin to grow next to each other. Both receive the same amount of water and sunlight. But one tree grows faster and taller than the other tree. Soon, the first tree grows so tall that it blocks out the sunlight for the other, smaller tree. After a while, the smaller tree can't get enough light to continue to grow. The smaller tree might not stay healthy. It might die before it becomes an adult tree.

A. Write <u>True</u> if the sentence is true. Write <u>False</u> if the sentence is false.

_______ 1. All plants that grow from the same parent plants are exactly alike.

_______ 2. The peaches from one peach tree can taste sweeter than the peaches from another peach tree.

_______ 3. When one tree grows faster than another tree, the first tree can block out the sunlight for the smaller tree.

B. Which tree shown here will probably live longer? Why?

____

____

____

____

C. Write one or more sentences to answer the question.

Two violet plants are growing next to each other. Both get enough sunlight. The plant on the right uses more water than the one on the left. But both plants are healthy and live a long time. What might be the reason for this?

____

____

CHAPTER 1

Watch a Seed Grow

You need:

• 5 seeds • 5 paper towels • tray • water

In this activity you will watch a seed grow.

Follow these steps:

1. Fold some paper towels. Put them on a tray. Spread the seeds on the paper towels. Cover the seeds with more paper towels.
2. Pour enough water on the paper towels to make them wet. Pour more water on the paper towels every day to keep them wet.
3. Watch to see what happens to the seeds.

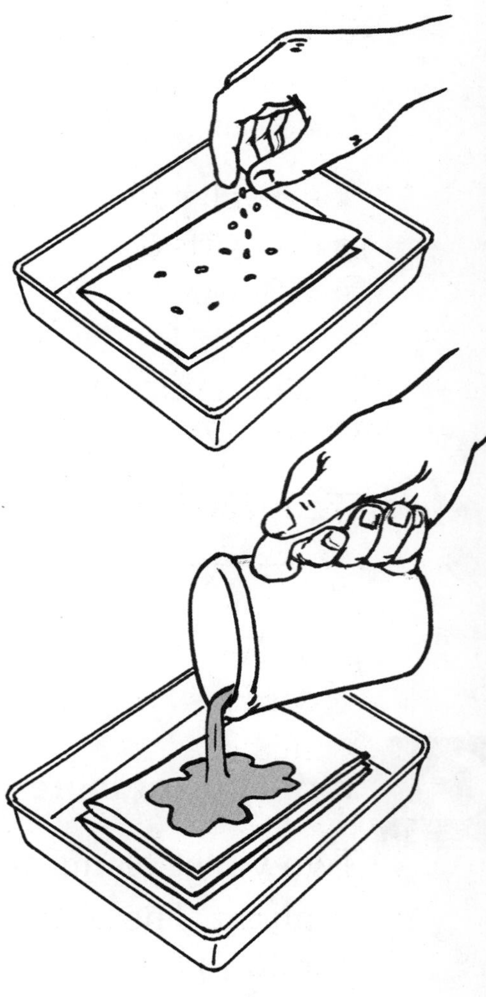

Write answers to these questions.

1. What two parts of the life cycle did you see in this activity?

___

___

___

2. How might the plants change over time if they were put into the ground?

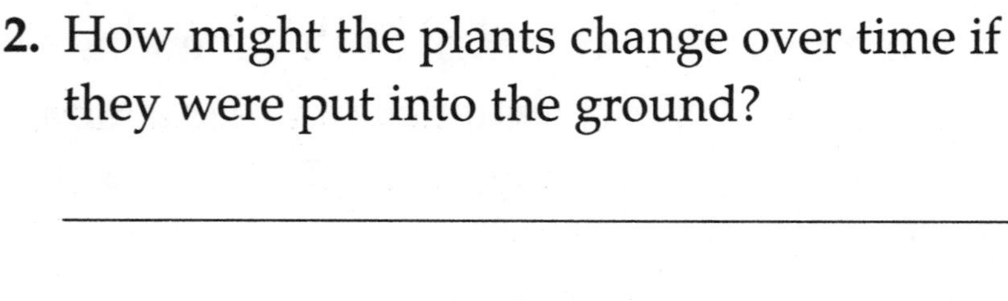

TEST CHAPTER 1

Darken the circle next to the correct answer.

1. What is the first part of the life cycle for most plants?
Ⓐ growing
Ⓑ being a seed
Ⓒ dying
Ⓓ adulthood

2. When plants are able to make new seeds, they are
Ⓐ thistles.
Ⓑ life cycles.
Ⓒ adults.
Ⓓ acorns.

3. The pistil, pollen, and stamen are all parts of
Ⓐ a flower.
Ⓑ a seed.
Ⓒ a life cycle.
Ⓓ an egg.

4. The fuzzy top of a stamen is covered with
Ⓐ pistil.
Ⓑ pollen.
Ⓒ seeds.
Ⓓ thistles.

5. How does pollen move from one plant to another?
Ⓐ pistils and stamen
Ⓑ rain and snow
Ⓒ wind and animals
Ⓓ sunlight and darkness

6. Flowers make a sweet juice called
Ⓐ pistil.
Ⓑ nectar.
Ⓒ thistle.
Ⓓ pollen.

7. The part of the plant that turns into a fruit is the
Ⓐ pollen.
Ⓑ stamen.
Ⓒ seed.
Ⓓ pistil.

8. When does a seed begin to grow?
Ⓐ when it is dry and cold
Ⓑ as soon as it leaves the fruit
Ⓒ when it is in wet, warm soil
Ⓓ as soon as it is formed

9. Why is it important for a seed to travel?
Ⓐ so that animals can get food
Ⓑ so that it can get enough water and sunlight
Ⓒ to get away from animals that eat it
Ⓓ to end its life cycle

10. Growing fast can help a new plant get enough
Ⓐ sunlight.
Ⓑ pollen.
Ⓒ wind.
Ⓓ nectar.

CHAPTER

2

The Life of Animals

Some animals, like these barn owls, need care from their parents when they are babies. Other young animals do well on their own. But all animals change and grow during their lives. A baby animal may look different from its mother and father. But when it is grown, it will look very much like its parents. In this chapter you'll learn about the way birds, butterflies, and other animals change as they grow.

- It is part of a butterfly's life cycle.
- It eats a lot.
- It is sometimes called a larva.

LESSON 1

What Is an Egg?

Every animal starts its life cycle as an egg. Elephants, spiders, fish, birds, and cats all begin as eggs. Not all eggs are the same, though. Some eggs are small. Many fish eggs are only about half the size of a letter on this page. The egg of a cat is too small to see. Other eggs can be large. Some birds lay eggs that are bigger than a softball.

A bird keeps its eggs safe and warm by sitting on them.

Animals like birds, turtles, and insects lay their eggs outside their bodies. Once the eggs are outside the animal's body, they need to be kept safe from harm. The eggs cannot get too hot or too cold. This is so the little animals inside can grow big and strong enough to stay alive outside their eggs.

Different animals have different ways of keeping their eggs safe. For example, chicken eggs and turtle eggs have tough shells to keep them safe. Many birds sit on their eggs to keep them warm. Turtles lay their eggs in a small hole where they will be safe and warm. Some spiders keep their eggs inside a small sack close to their bodies.

The cat's eggs grow into kittens inside the cat's body.

Some animals keep their eggs inside their bodies. Cats, dogs, rabbits, and squirrels all grow from eggs inside their mothers' bodies. That way, the new animals can be kept safe and warm until they are strong enough to leave their mothers' bodies.

A. Write True if the sentence is true. Write False if the sentence is false.

______ 1. All animals begin as eggs.

______ 2. All eggs look exactly alike.

______ 3. Some animals lay their eggs outside their bodies.

______ 4. Some animals keep their eggs inside their bodies.

B. Write Outside after the name of each animal that lays its eggs outside its body. Write Inside after the name of each animal that keeps its eggs inside its body.

1. chicken ______________________
2. cat ______________________
3. turtle ______________________
4. rabbit ______________________
5. spider ______________________
6. squirrel ______________________

C. Write one or more sentences to answer the question.

After a turtle lays its eggs in a small hole in the ground, it covers them up. Why do you think the turtle does this?

____

____

____

____

____

LESSON 2 Do Animals Look Like Their Parents?

A baby animal grows up to look a lot like its mother and father. But there are always some differences. When a white cat with black spots and an orange cat have kittens, each kitten will look like a tiny cat. Some of the kittens might be black and white. But some might be orange. Some might even be white with black and orange spots. Some of the kittens might grow up to be bigger or smaller than their parents. Some might have tails that are longer than those of their parents.

When a blue jay lays eggs, all of the baby birds will look like blue jays. Some of the baby birds might grow up with stronger wings and bigger bodies than those of their parents. Others might have shorter legs.

The same thing happens when two people have children. Many children look like their mothers or fathers. But no child ever looks exactly like his or her parents. Two tall parents with brown eyes and brown hair might have a tall child who has brown hair and blue eyes. The same parents might have a short child who has brown eyes and brown hair. There are many ways in which children may look like their mothers or fathers. They might have the same kind of smile. They might have the same shaped chin, hands, knees, or ears. But there are just as many ways for children to look different from their mothers or fathers.

These kittens look like cats. But the kitten in the middle might grow up to be bigger than its mother or father.

A. Underline the correct word or words in each sentence.

1. Baby animals grow up to look (a lot, exactly) like their parents.
2. When two dogs become parents, (all, some) of the puppies will look like dogs.
3. It is (possible, impossible) for a baby blue jay to be bigger and stronger than its parents when it grows up.
4. There are (many, only a few) ways that children can look different from their parents.

B. Write one way that each animal might be different from its parents when it grows up.

1. puppy

____

2. baby spider

____

3. baby blue jay

____

C. Write one or more sentences to answer the question.

In a family of four puppies, one is bigger and stronger than the others. How might being bigger and stronger help this puppy?

____

____

____

____

____

LESSON

3 How Do Birds Change?

As a robin grows and becomes an adult, it will grow red feathers on its chest. A swan will grow a long neck and snowy white wings. But every bird, from a robin to a swan, goes through the same kinds of changes during its life cycle.

A baby swan does not look very much like an adult swan.

Most birds build a **nest** just before they become parents. A nest is a home for baby birds. Eagles build large nests high on cliffs. Swallows build small nests inside barns.

When the nest is built, the mother bird will lay eggs in it. While the baby birds grow inside the eggs, the parents guard the eggs and keep them warm. When the birds grow strong enough, they break through their shells. This is how all birds are born.

All bird nests are homes for baby birds.

Most new birds cannot fly or get food. They do not look much like their parents yet. The parents bring them food and keep them safe. Baby birds spend a few weeks in their nests, eating and growing.

As the babies grow, they begin to look more like their parents. One day, they are strong enough to leave the nest and take care of themselves. When they grow into adult birds, they can make nests and raise their own new babies. After a bird raises several families of new birds, it grows old and dies. But its babies grow up and have their own families. That way, the life cycle keeps going.

A. Write True if the sentence is true. Write False if the sentence is false.

_______ 1. All birds go through the same kinds of changes during their life cycles.

_______ 2. All birds build the same size nests.

_______ 3. Nests are homes for baby birds.

_______ 4. Eagles build small nests inside barns.

_______ 5. When baby birds are ready to be born, their parents break their eggs for them.

_______ 6. When they are born, baby birds look just like their parents.

_______ 7. When baby birds are born, they can fly and get their own food.

B. The sentences below tell about birds. Write 1, 2, 3, and 4 to show the correct order.

_______ The parent birds feed their babies.

_______ Two birds build a nest.

_______ The baby birds are ready to fly from the nest.

_______ The parent birds guard the eggs.

C. Write one or more sentences to answer the question.

Why do you think birds build their nests high in trees or on cliffs?

____

____

____

____

LESSON

4 How Do Butterflies Change?

Like birds, different kinds of butterflies go through the same changes during their life cycles. A butterfly starts as an egg. When it comes out of the egg, it is a **larva**. A butterfly larva is also called a **caterpillar**. Next, the larva becomes a **pupa**, which finally turns into a butterfly.

A female butterfly lays eggs on a plant that will give her babies food. Inside each egg, a larva grows. As soon as the larva comes out of the egg, it begins to eat the plant. The larva does not look like its parents at all. It is a caterpillar with many legs and no wings. It is like an eating machine. The job of the larva is to eat and grow.

When the larva grows to its full size, it changes into a pupa. The pupa has a hard covering. The pupa hangs from a leaf or branch. This is the third part of the life cycle. The pupa does not look like a butterfly yet. But inside the hard covering, the pupa is changing into an adult butterfly.

When the butterfly is finished growing, it breaks out of the hard covering. Now the butterfly finally looks like its parents. And if it is a female butterfly, it can lay eggs. Most kinds of butterflies live for one or two weeks. But even if a butterfly dies, the eggs it has laid start the life cycle all over again.

Life Cycle of a Butterfly

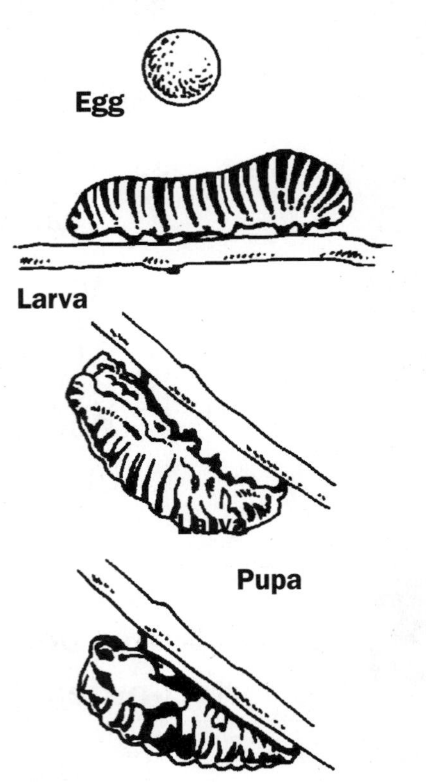

Adult breaks out of hard covering.

Adult flies away.

A.

The sentences below tell how a butterfly is born. Write 1, 2, 3, 4, and 5 to show the correct order. The first one is done for you.

_______ **1.** An adult butterfly comes out of its hard covering.

___1___ **2.** A butterfly lays eggs on a plant.

_______ **3.** The larva eats the leaves of the plant.

_______ **4.** A larva breaks out of an egg.

_______ **5.** The larva changes into a pupa.

B.

Write True if the sentence is true. Write False if the sentence is false.

_______ **1.** A butterfly larva is a caterpillar.

_______ **2.** A larva can lay eggs.

_______ **3.** A larva looks like its parents.

_______ **4.** The job of a larva is to eat and grow.

_______ **5.** All butterflies grow inside a pupa.

_______ **6.** A pupa moves around as it eats.

_______ **7.** Most kinds of butterflies live for one or two weeks.

C.

Write one or more sentences to answer the question.

The butterfly larva saves much of the food it eats in its body. What do you think happens to this food?

____

____

____

____

____

How Do Fish, Amphibians, and Reptiles Change?

All kinds of animals have life cycles that are the same in some ways and different in other ways. Fish and other animals have their own life cycles, too.

Like all animals, fish start as eggs. Most fish lay eggs outside their bodies. A single adult fish can lay hundreds of eggs at a time under the water. Fish eggs are soft and tiny. Once the baby fish come out of the eggs, they do not need a parent to take care of them. A baby fish can swim away as soon as it is born. Over time, it grows bigger and becomes an adult fish.

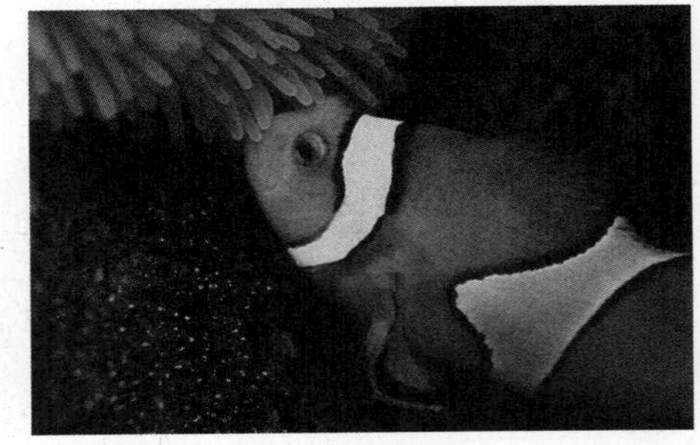

Fish can lay hundreds of eggs at a time.

An **amphibian** is an animal, such as a frog, that lives both in water and on dry land. Like fish, frogs lay many eggs at a time under the water. Frog eggs are also soft and tiny. The animal that comes out of a frog egg looks more like a fish than a frog. It is called a **tadpole**. A tadpole can live only in water. Little by little, it grows legs and loses its tail. It becomes an adult frog that can live on dry land and lay eggs.

Life Cycle of a Frog

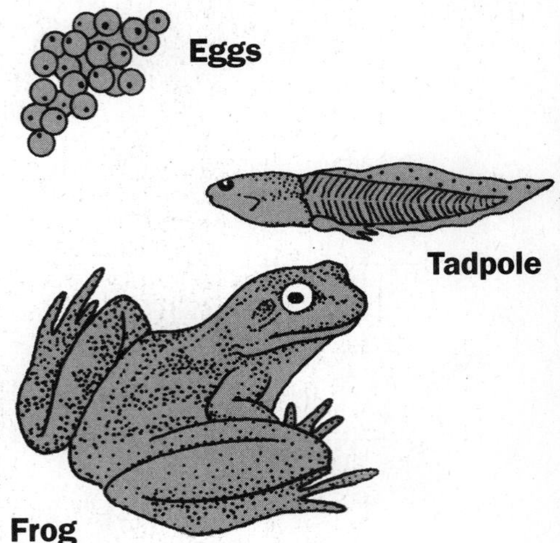

A **reptile** lays its eggs on dry land. A reptile lays eggs that have hard shells. Most reptiles are able to take care of themselves once they leave the eggs. Turtles and snakes are reptiles.

A. Write the word that best completes each sentence.

amphibians **eggs** **fish** **reptiles** **tadpole**

1. Fish lay hundreds of ______________________ under the water.
2. Frogs are ______________________ because they live in water and on land.
3. When a baby frog comes out of its egg, it looks like a ______________________.
4. As it becomes an adult, a ______________________ grows legs and loses its tail.
5. Baby ______________________ come out of eggs on dry land and look like their parents.

B. Each picture shows one part of the life cycle of a frog. Write 1, 2, and 3 under each picture to show the correct order.

________ ________ ________

C. Write one or more sentences to answer the question.

How are amphibians different from fish and reptiles in the way they become adults?

____

____

LESSON

6 How Do Mammals Change?

Squirrels, dogs, lions, bears, and humans are a few kinds of animals called **mammals**. Like birds, fish, and reptiles, mammals also go through changes during their life cycles.

A mammal's life cycle has four parts. Like all animals, mammals start as an egg. But, almost all mammal eggs grow into baby animals inside the mother's body. Growing from an egg into a baby is the first part of a mammal's life cycle.

Human babies need their parents to take care of them.

After a mammal is born, it needs a lot of care. Its mother feeds it milk from her body. This is called **nursing**. It is the second part of a mammal's life cycle. During nursing, mammals learn many things they need to know to take care of themselves. Mammals like dogs and cats nurse only for a few weeks. Elephants nurse for years. Human babies might nurse for a year, but they still need adults to care for them for many years.

All mammals nurse their young.

Mammals keep growing after they stop nursing. The time when they are growing into adults is the third part of a mammal's life cycle. It takes some mammals years to become adults. The fourth part of a mammal's life cycle is when it becomes an adult. Once a mammal is an adult, it can make baby mammals. Then, the life cycle begins again.

A. Write <u>True</u> if the sentence is true. Write <u>False</u> if the sentence is false.

________ 1. Most mammals keep their eggs inside them until the eggs grow into baby animals.

________ 2. All mammals nurse their young with milk.

________ 3. Mammals have a life cycle that has six parts.

________ 4. After they are born, mammals need a lot of care.

B. Write the word that best completes each sentence.

adults	grows	milk	years

1. Some mammals, like humans, grow for many

   ____________________ before they become adults.

2. During the second part of a mammal's life cycle, it

   ____________________.

3. As soon as a baby mammal is born, it needs

   ____________________ from its mother.

4. Mammals can make baby mammals when they become

   ____________________.

C. Write one or more sentences to answer the questions.

How is the life cycle of a cat like that of a human? How is it different?

____

____

____

____

CHAPTER 2

Model a Life Cycle

You need:

- **green clay**

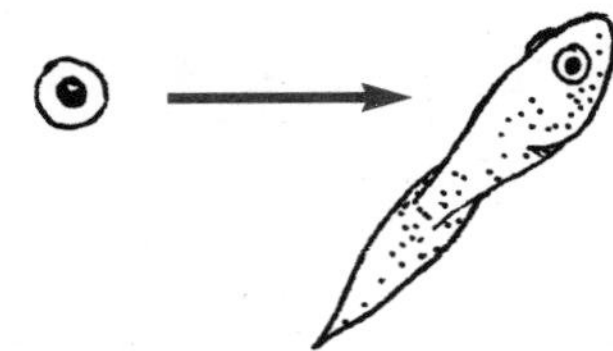

In this activity you will model the life cycle of a frog. Use the pictures to help you make your model.

Follow these steps:

1. Use some clay to make a model of a frog egg.
2. Add clay to your model of a frog egg to make a model of a baby tadpole.
3. Add legs to your model of a tadpole.
4. Take the tail off of your tadpole. Add more clay to the model to make it into a frog.

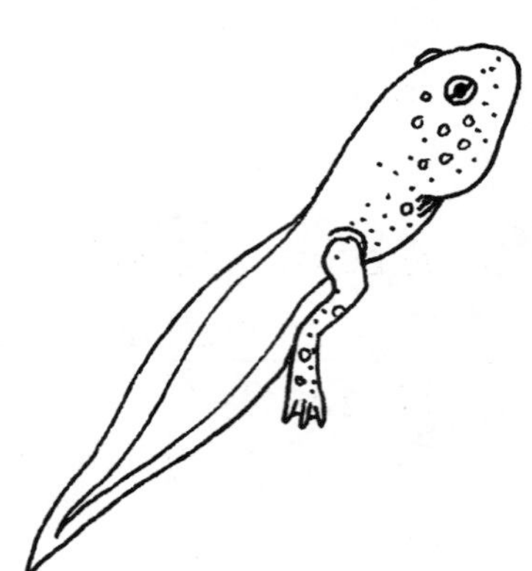

Write answers to these questions.

1. What parts of a frog life cycle did you model?

____

____

____

2. How can an adult frog start a new life cycle?

____

____

TEST CHAPTER 2

Darken the circle next to the correct answer.

1. Every animal starts out as
   Ⓐ a larva.
   Ⓑ a fish.
   Ⓒ an egg.
   Ⓓ a pupa.

2. Which of these animals lays eggs outside of its body?
   Ⓐ dog
   Ⓑ chicken
   Ⓒ human
   Ⓓ squirrel

3. A baby animal grows up to look like its parents, but it will always be a little
   Ⓐ child.
   Ⓑ stronger.
   Ⓒ different.
   Ⓓ shorter.

4. Where do most birds lay their eggs?
   Ⓐ in nests
   Ⓑ in holes in the ground
   Ⓒ under the water
   Ⓓ in trees

5. When a butterfly is first born, it is a
   Ⓐ pupa.
   Ⓑ butterfly.
   Ⓒ egg.
   Ⓓ larva.

6. What does a larva turn into?
   Ⓐ an egg
   Ⓑ a bigger larva
   Ⓒ a pupa
   Ⓓ an adult butterfly

7. A tadpole can live only
   Ⓐ in water.
   Ⓑ with no legs.
   Ⓒ near a frog.
   Ⓓ on dry land.

8. Where do snakes lay their eggs?
   Ⓐ in trees
   Ⓑ under the water
   Ⓒ under the ground
   Ⓓ on dry land

9. What is the first part of a mammal's life cycle?
   Ⓐ nursing
   Ⓑ becoming a pupa
   Ⓒ growing from an egg into a baby
   Ⓓ being an adult

10. What do mammals feed their babies when they are born?
   Ⓐ milk
   Ⓑ seeds
   Ⓒ water
   Ⓓ fruit

CHAPTER

3

Bones and Muscles

Without bones and muscles, the girls in this picture could not dance. Even if you are not a dancer, bones and muscles are important parts of your body. Without them you could not move or live. How do bones and muscles work? How can dancing make them stronger? What are some other ways to keep bones and muscles healthy? You will learn the answers to these questions in this chapter.

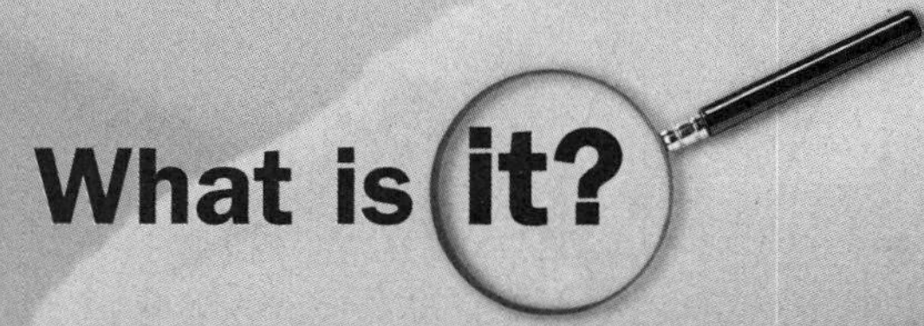

- **It comes from the foods you eat.**
- **Your body uses it to run and think.**
- **It is power.**

What Is a Skeleton?

What do you think holds your body up? Your body is held together by your **skeleton**. You can't see your skeleton because it holds you up from the inside.

Human skeletons are made of **bones**. Human skeletons have more than two hundred bones! You can feel your bones through your skin. Bones are hard on the outside and soft on the inside. The soft inside part of bones is called **bone marrow**.

Some tough parts of your body are made of **cartilage**. Cartilage is not as hard as bone, but it is strong. Cartilage can also bend. The outside parts of your ears are made of cartilage. So is the tip of your nose. Some bones have cartilage on their ends. The cartilage helps keep those bones from rubbing against each other.

There are many kinds of bones in your body. Bones can be many shapes and sizes. Some bones are very small. Other bones are much bigger.

The picture shows some kinds of bones in your body. Most of the bones in your head are part of your **skull**. In your chest, you have many bones called **ribs**. The small bones that run down the middle of your back are part of your **spine**. The bones in your arms and legs are called **long bones**.

A Human Skeleton

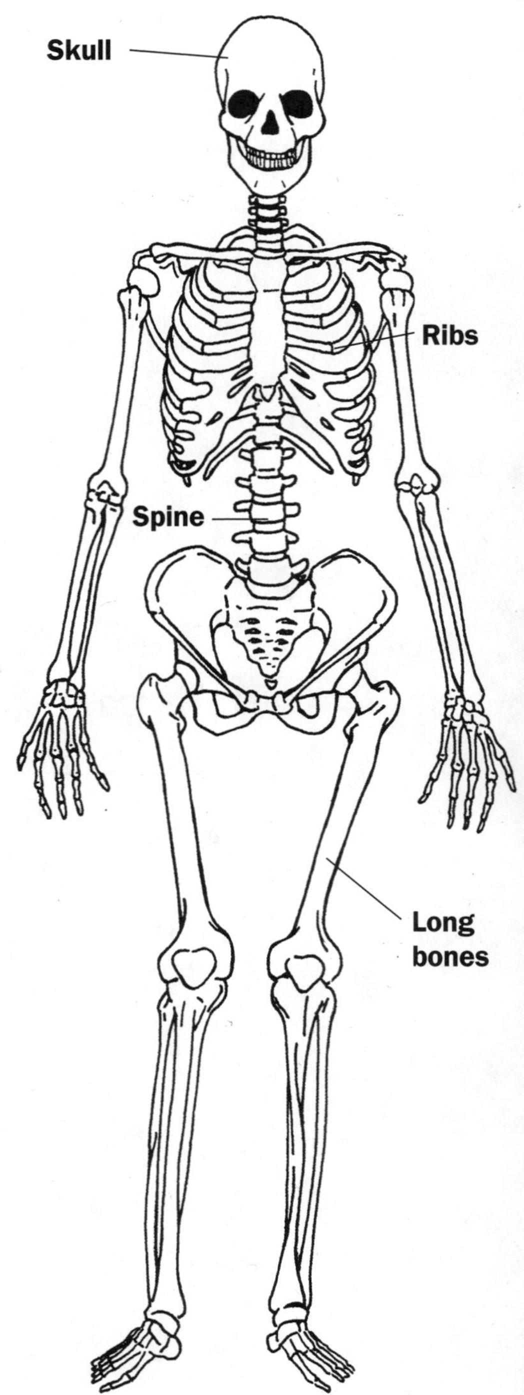

A. Write True if the sentence is true. Write False if the sentence is false.

_________ **1.** Your skeleton is made of bones.

_________ **2.** Bones are hard all the way through.

_________ **3.** Cartilage keeps some bones from rubbing against each other.

_________ **4.** All bones are the same size and shape.

_________ **5.** The bones in your head are called ribs.

B. Write a sentence to answer each question.

1. How is the inside of bones different from the outside?

____

____

____

2. What can cartilage do that bones cannot do?

____

____

____

C. Write one or more sentences to answer the questions.

Look at the picture of the human skeleton on page 40. What parts of your body do you think have small bones? What parts do you think have long bones?

____

____

____

____

LESSON 2

Where Do Bones Join?

When people move, their bones move, too. People can even move so that one bone goes one way and another bone goes a different way. Why do you think people can do that? The human body can move that way because of places called **joints**. Joints are the places where your bones meet each other.

Most joints can move. There are different kinds of joints that can move. **Hinge joints** work like the hinge on a door. They let bones move back and forth. Knees and elbows are hinge joints. Elbows are also **pivot joints**, which let bones turn and twist. People use the pivot joints in their elbows when they open jars or bottles.

Shoulders have **ball and socket joints**. Ball and socket joints allow one bone to be moved in a circle while the other stays still. Swimmers use the ball and socket joints in their shoulders when they swim.

The small bones in your spine are joined by **sliding joints**. Sliding joints allow turning and bending. Without sliding joints in their spines, people could not bend over to touch their toes.

Some joints, called **fixed joints**, don't help you to move around. Bones that meet at fixed joints stay in one place. The bones in your skull are held together at fixed joints.

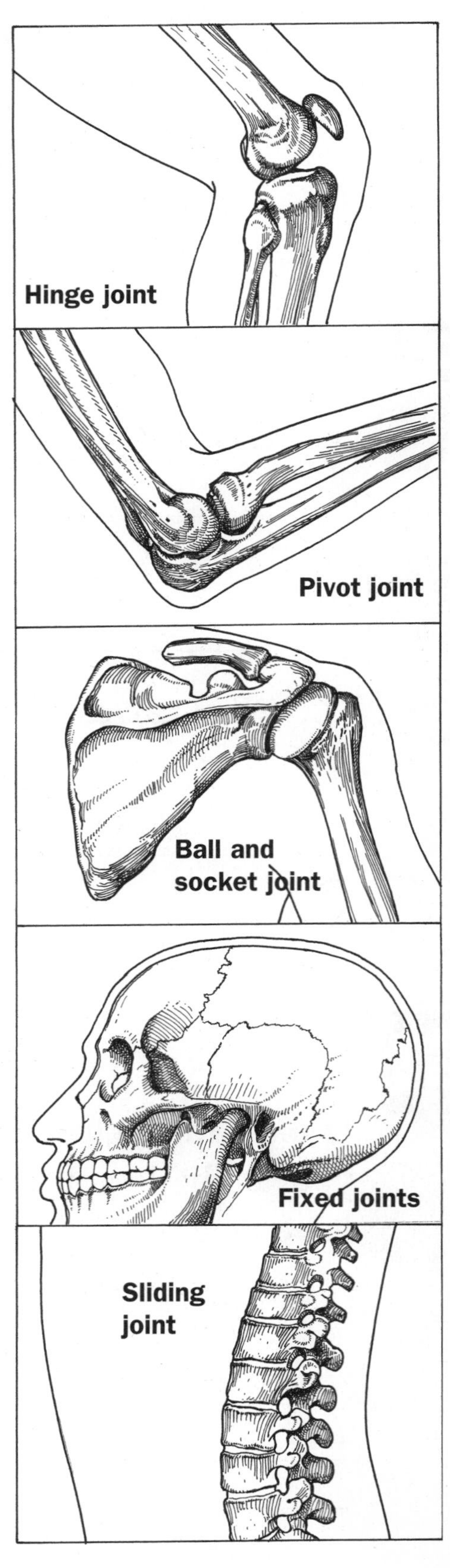

A. Write the missing word or words in each sentence.

1. An elbow is a ______________________ joint. (moving, fixed)

2. Pivot joints let bones ______________________. (turn and twist, move in circles)

3. There is a ball and socket joint in your ______________________. (shoulder, elbow)

4. People can bend over and touch their toes because of the ______________________ joints in the spine. (pivot, sliding)

B. Draw a line from each kind of joint to one place on the skeleton that uses that kind of joint.

Hinge joint

Pivot joint

Ball and socket joint

Sliding joint

Fixed joint

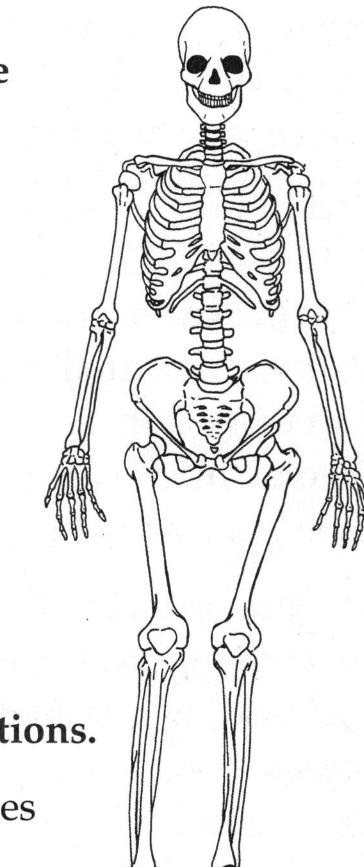

C. Write one or more sentences to answer the questions.

Suppose that people had fixed joints in their spines instead of sliding joints. Could they move just as easily? Why or why not?

____

____

LESSON 3

What Do Muscles Do?

As you have learned, your bones can be moved in different ways because you have joints. But your bones can't move themselves. Only **muscles** can make bones move. People have to use muscles every time they move. You even have to use muscles every time you blink your eyes!

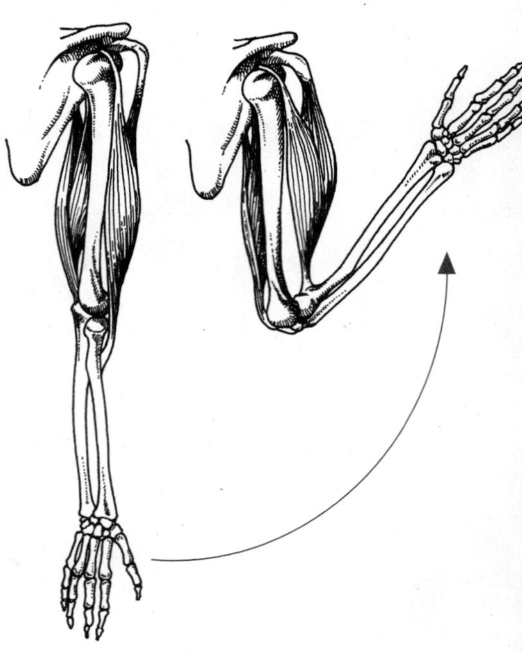

A muscle is long when it rests. When a muscle works, it gets short and round.

Muscles work by pulling themselves into a short, round shape. Look at the picture of an arm muscle. When the muscle rests, it is long. When it works, it gets short and round.

What do you think happens to your bones when your muscles work? Your muscles are tied to your bones by long, thin bands called **tendons**. Tendons are strong and they stretch. When your muscle pulls into a short, round shape, it also pulls tendons. The tendons are tied to the bone, so the muscle pulls the bone when it moves.

Muscles can only pull in one direction when they move. They can't push. That means that the same muscle can't pull a bone one way and then push it back again. A different muscle has to pull the bone back. Because each muscle can only pull one way, people have to use lots of muscles every time they move. Moving your hand and fingers uses about 20 muscles. When you walk, you use more than 100 muscles!

A. Place a ✔ next to the ways people use muscles.

_________ 1. smile

_________ 2. walk

_________ 3. think

_________ 4. talk

_________ 5. listen

_________ 6. eat

B. Draw a line to complete each sentence.

1. Only muscles can	to bones.
2. Muscles work by	cause bones to move.
3. Tendons tie muscles	getting short and round.

C. Write the correct labels under the pictures.

Muscle at rest

Muscle at work

_________________________ _________________________

D. Write one or more sentences to answer the questions.

In what part of your body are your longest muscles? Why?

____

____

LESSON 4 What Is the Heart?

Your **heart** has the strongest muscles in your body. Your heart does not make your bones move. Instead, it makes **blood** move to all the different parts of your body. Your heart is very important. Without your heart, you could not stay alive.

Your heart is about the same size as your fist. It has space inside for blood to move through it. Your heart muscles are different from other muscles. You can make most of your muscles work or stop working. Your heart is different because it works on its own. To move blood, muscles in your heart squeeze together. This is called a **heartbeat**.

What would happen if you were holding a balloon full of water and then squeezed it? The water would squeeze out. The same thing happens when your heart beats. Blood squeezes out. Each time your heart beats, more blood squeezes out. The blood that squeezes out pushes the blood in front of it. Moving this way, your blood travels all around your body. It carries food and air to all the parts of your body. Then, it comes back to your heart.

As you can see, your heart has a very important job to do. No matter what you do, your heart beats all the time and never stops or gets tired.

The Heart

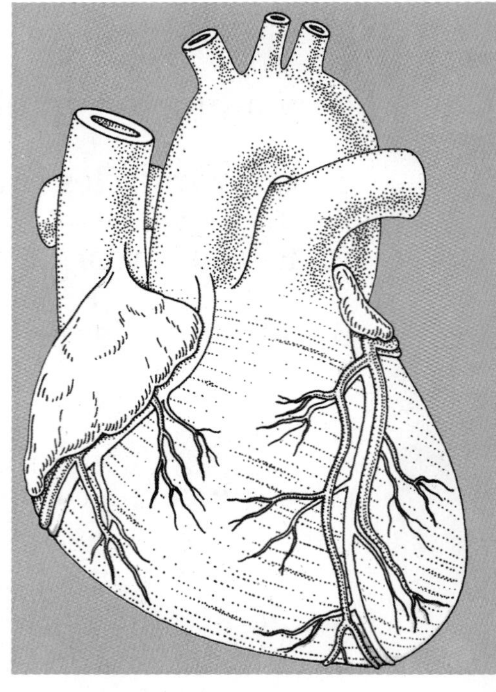

Your heart makes blood move to all the parts of your body.

A. Write the missing word or words in each sentence.

1. Your heart has the strongest ______________________ in your body.
   (muscles, blood, tendons)

2. Your heart makes your ______________________ move.
   (tendons, blood, muscles)

3. Your blood carries ______________________ to all the parts of your body.
   (tendons, muscles, food and air)

B. Write True if the sentence is true. Write False if the sentence is false.

________ 1. You could stay alive even if your heart stopped beating.

________ 2. A heartbeat happens when your heart muscles squeeze together.

________ 3. Your heart beats all the time and never stops or gets tired.

C. List three ways that make your heart muscles different from other muscles.

1. ____

2. ____

3. ____

D. Write one or more sentences to answer the question.

Why do you think it is important for your heart to work on its own no matter what you do?

____

____

How Can You Stay Healthy?

You must take care of your bones and muscles so they will be healthy. Healthy bones and muscles can grow strong. One way to take care of your bones and muscles is to exercise every day. Walking, running, playing ball, and dancing are all good ways to exercise. Sitting and watching television are not. What are some other ways to exercise?

Exercise helps your bones. When you exercise, muscles press on your bones. This pressing is a signal for your body to send more **calcium** to your bones. Calcium is what makes your bones hard and strong.

When you run, walk, ride a bike, or swim, you move many muscles. You move muscles in your arms, legs, and back. Moving these muscles makes them stronger. The more you exercise, the stronger your muscles will get.

When you exercise, your heart beats faster. It moves your blood around faster. When blood moves faster, it can carry more food and air to all the parts of your body. This makes your body healthy.

Another way to take care of your muscles and bones is to get plenty of sleep. When you are asleep, your bones and muscles rest. Your body repairs them. Your body also does a lot of growing while you sleep.

Exercise

Exercise makes your heart, muscles, and bones strong and healthy.

A. Put a ✔ next to the ways exercise helps your bones and muscles.

________ **1.** Exercise makes muscles stronger.

________ **2.** Exercise gives your body time to fix your bones and muscles.

________ **3.** Exercise can make your body send more calcium to your bones.

________ **4.** Exercise causes your heart to send more food and air to all the parts of your body.

________ **5.** Exercise lets your bones and muscles rest.

B. Write the missing word or words in each sentence.

1. Exercise makes your heart beat ____________________ .
(faster, slower, stay the same)

2. Calcium makes your ____________________ harder.
(tendons, bones, muscles)

3. Sleeping lets your bones and muscles ____________________ .
(work harder, rest, get stronger)

C. Write one or more sentences to answer the question.

Would you get more exercise playing soccer or playing kickball? Explain why.

____

____

____

____

____

LESSON 6 What Other Ways Can You Stay Healthy?

Eating the right foods is the best way to take care of your bones and muscles. Your body needs power to run, jump, and think. This power is called **energy**. It comes from food. Your body also uses food to grow and repair itself. You should eat foods that give you energy and help you to grow.

The Food Pyramid

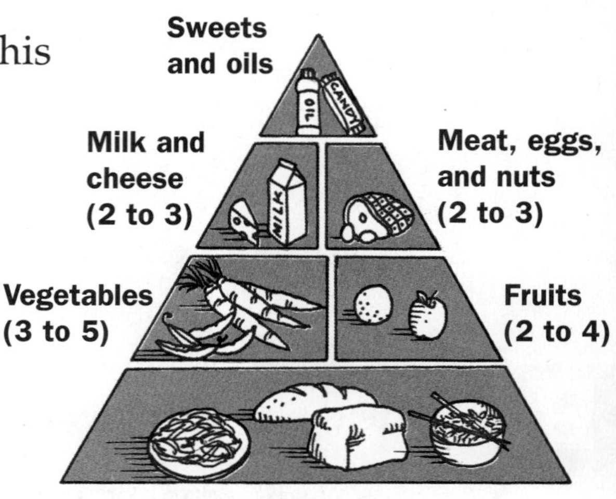

The numbers show how many helpings you should eat every day. Do not eat a lot of sweets and oils.

The picture on this page is called the **food pyramid**. Each part of the pyramid has a different kind of food. The biggest part of the pyramid shows the kinds of foods you should eat most often. These foods give your body energy. They are foods like bread, rice, and noodles. You should also eat plenty of vegetables and fruits. Find them on the pyramid. They give you energy, too.

Foods like milk and meat are right above fruits and vegetables in the pyramid. Milk and meat are like building blocks. Milk and meat help your body grow and repair itself.

The foods shown in the lower five parts of the pyramid also have **vitamins** and **minerals**. Vitamins and minerals help your body grow and stay healthy. Calcium is a mineral in milk and some vegetables. Vitamin C in fruits and vegetables may help keep you from getting sick.

Watch out for sweets and oils at the tip of the pyramid! You should not eat a lot of sweets and oils.

A. Write the missing word or words in each sentence.

1. To help your body stay healthy, you should

   ______________________ .

   (play video games, eat the right foods)

2. The power your body needs to stay alive is called

   ______________________ .

   (food pyramid, energy)

3. Foods like bread, fruits, and vegetables give your body the

   ______________________ that it needs.

   (energy, milk)

4. Vitamin C can keep you from ______________________ .

   (getting sick, eating right)

B. Write the name of each food where it belongs in the food pyramid.

apple	chicken
bread	milk
candy	peanut
carrot	rice

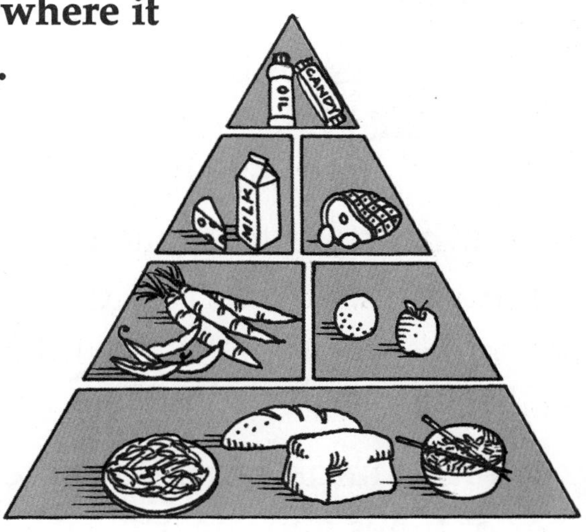

C. Write one or more sentences to answer the question.

The bottom part of the food pyramid is much larger than the tip. What does this tell you about how much food you should eat from each of these parts?

____

____

CHAPTER 3

Listen to Your Heart

You need:

- **stopwatch or clock with a second hand**
- **pencil**

In this activity you will count your heartbeats.

Follow these steps:

1. Put your fingers on your wrist so that you can feel your heartbeat.
2. Count the number of times your heart beats in one minute. Write the number here. ________
3. Do jumping jacks for one minute. Go as fast as you can! Then, put your fingers on your wrist again. Count the number of times your heart beats in one minute. Write the number here. ________

Write answers to these questions.

1. How did the jumping jacks change the number of times your heart beat?

____

2. Do you think your heart beats faster when you are walking or sleeping? Why?

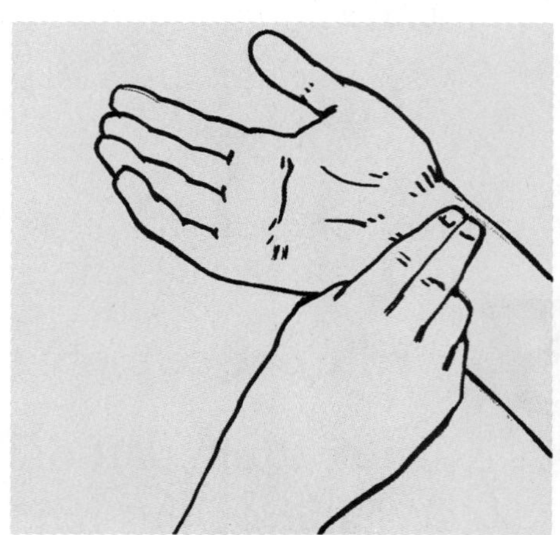

____

____

TEST CHAPTER 3

Darken the circle next to the correct answer.

1. Your skeleton is made of
   Ⓐ cartilage.
   Ⓑ muscles.
   Ⓒ bones.
   Ⓓ tendons.

2. The bones that run down your back are called your
   Ⓐ ribs.
   Ⓑ spine.
   Ⓒ long bones.
   Ⓓ skull.

3. Which kind of joints are found in your skull?
   Ⓐ fixed
   Ⓑ hinge
   Ⓒ ball and socket
   Ⓓ sliding

4. What makes your bones move?
   Ⓐ joints
   Ⓑ tendons
   Ⓒ muscles
   Ⓓ cartilage

5. Your muscles are attached to your bones by
   Ⓐ joints.
   Ⓑ tendons.
   Ⓒ ribs.
   Ⓓ cartilage.

6. How is your heart different from the muscles that move your bones?
   Ⓐ It can push and pull.
   Ⓑ It beats on its own.
   Ⓒ It stops when you make it.
   Ⓓ It gets tired often.

7. What does your heart send all around your body?
   Ⓐ muscles
   Ⓑ cartilage
   Ⓒ bones
   Ⓓ blood

8. Which activity is good for your bones and muscles?
   Ⓐ watching television
   Ⓑ exercising
   Ⓒ reading
   Ⓓ eating sweets

9. What does the mineral calcium do for your body?
   Ⓐ It makes your muscles rest.
   Ⓑ It keeps you from getting sick.
   Ⓒ It makes your bones hard and strong.
   Ⓓ It gives you energy.

10. The power your body needs to stay alive is called
   Ⓐ energy.
   Ⓑ muscles.
   Ⓒ tendons.
   Ⓓ sleep.

Careers

Plant Breeder

People need to grow plants for food. A plant breeder helps by working to make plants stronger. Plant breeders also make plants that grow faster and are better for people to eat.

Plant breeders use the seeds from the best plants. Sometimes they mix two kinds of plants together to make a new and better plant. Corn is a plant that breeders have made better over the years.

Beekeeper

Why would people want to keep bees? A beekeeper would because bees make honey and wax. Some beekeepers keep bees to study them and how they work. Other beekeepers sell the honey and the wax. They take good care of bees in boxes called hives.

Beekeepers wear special clothes and hats so the bees won't sting them. Beekeepers handle the bees carefully when they collect the honey and wax.

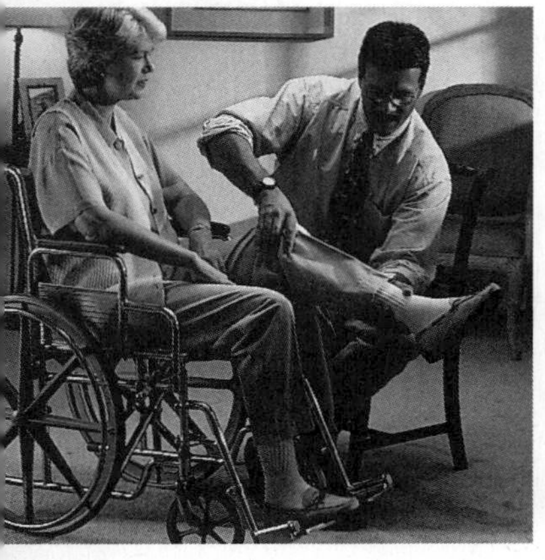

Physical Therapist

A physical therapist uses heat, cold, light, and exercise to treat people who get hurt or sick. Exercise helps to make people stronger. It also helps them to move around more easily. Physical therapists work in clinics, hospitals, nursing homes, and other places.

A. Write the missing word or words in each sentence.

1. Plants get food to live and grow ______________________ .
   (from animals, by making it, by eating)

2. To make food, a green plant needs water, light, and
   ______________________ .
   (air, darkness, dirt)

3. A plant makes food in its ______________________ .
   (leaves, roots, sugar)

4. Water enters the roots and moves up the
   ______________________ to the leaves.
   (sugar, soil, stem)

5. Light from the ______________________ makes air and water join to form food.
   (sun, leaves, soil)

B. The sentences below tell how plants make food. Write 1, 2, and 3 to show the correct order.

________ Air and water come into the leaves.

________ The plant sends food to its roots for storage.

________ Light changes air and water to food.

C. Write one or more sentences to answer the questions.

You have a plant in a pot. Where is the best place to put the plant in a room? Why?

____

____

____

LESSON 2 How Do Animals Get Food?

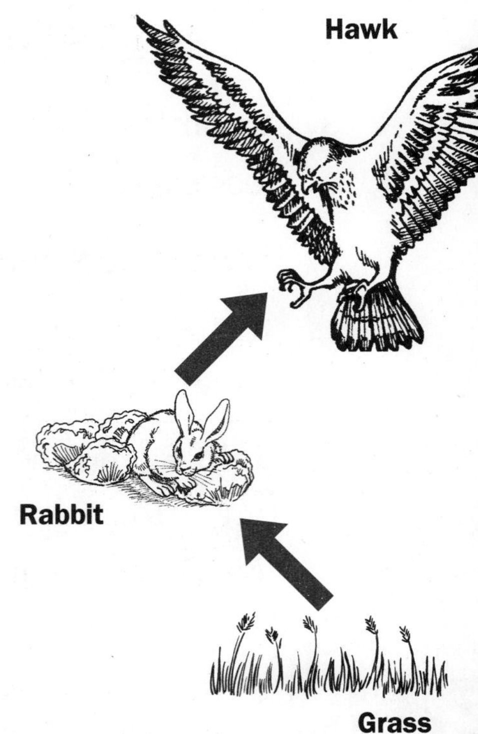

Like plants, animals get energy from food. As you know, plants make their own food. Animals cannot make food. They have to find food. Some animals use plants for food. We call them **plant-eaters**. Other animals eat these plant-eaters. We call them **animal-eaters**.

Plants and animals are joined like **links**, or parts, in a chain. This chain is called a **food chain**. One living thing makes or uses food and then becomes food for the next living thing. At each step, energy passes from one living thing to another.

A food chain begins with plants. For example, grass makes its own food and uses it to grow. It stores energy.

Plant-eaters come next in this food chain. A rabbit hops up and begins eating the grass. This food gives the rabbit energy to live and grow. The energy from the grass now becomes part of the rabbit.

Where does the energy in the rabbit go? It goes into an animal-eater. One day a hawk flies over a field. It sees the rabbit and dives down to catch it. The hawk eats the rabbit and gets energy from it. But no animal hunts hawks to eat. This food chain ends with the hawk. Each living thing in this food chain has taken energy from outside itself to live.

A. Write the word or words that best complete each sentence.

animal-eaters	**food chain**	**plants**
energy	**plant-eaters**	

1. Energy passes as food from one living thing to another in a ____________________.
2. Energy in ____________________ is stored as food.
3. Plants are eaten by animals called ____________________.
4. Animals that eat other animals are called ____________________.
5. By eating food, animals get ____________________ to live and grow.

B. Draw a line from the animal to the food it eats. Then, write plant-eater or animal-eater in the blank.

1. hawk leaves ____________________
2. deer mice ____________________

C. Write one or more sentences to answer the question.

How does the energy stored in grass get to a hawk?

____

____

____

____

____

LESSON 3 What Are Decomposers?

Sooner or later, all living things die. What happens when a plant or an animal dies? Its body begins to break down into small pieces. Special living things called **decomposers** break down the body.

Mushrooms are growing on a dead tree. They get energy from the wood as they break it down.

Some worms and mushrooms are decomposers. The worms live in the ground. They eat their way through bits of dead plants and animals. Some mushrooms grow out of the dead plants and animals and help break them down. But most decomposers are too small for us to see. They are all around us in the air and in the ground.

When a rabbit dies, decomposers begin to work. The rabbit's body is made up of bone, muscle, fur, blood, and other parts. Decomposers break these parts into smaller and smaller pieces. As they work, the decomposers get energy from the rabbit's body. Then, they let very small pieces that they cannot use into the air and the ground.

Over some weeks, the body of the rabbit seems to disappear. But the tiny pieces of it in the air and in the ground help plants live and grow. Every part of the rabbit is used again.

If dead plants and animals did not break down, Earth would be covered with their bodies. We need decomposers. They keep Earth clean and help plants grow.

A. Write <u>True</u> if the sentence is true. Write <u>False</u> if the sentence is false.

________ **1.** Every living thing dies and breaks down.

________ **2.** Some worms and mushrooms are decomposers.

________ **3.** Decomposers break down bodies into smaller pieces.

________ **4.** All decomposers are large enough for us to see.

________ **5.** It may take weeks for decomposers to break down a body.

B. Write 1, 2, and 3 to show what happens first, second, and last.

________ Decomposers let what they cannot use into the air and ground.

________ Decomposers start to break the tree down.

________ A dead tree falls to the forest floor.

C. Write one or more sentences to answer the question.

Decomposers help give us the plants we eat. How?

____

____

____

____

____

LESSON 4

What Other Ways Do Animals Use Plants?

Animals use plants for more than just food. Many animals use plants to build their homes. They also use plants for safety.

A squirrel builds its home high in a tree. It may find a hole in the trunk. It may find a place in the leaves of the tree. It uses leaves to make a nest. The squirrel stays warm in winter and raises its young in the nest.

A bird finds a safe branch in the same tree. She brings small branches and grass to make a nest. This is where she lays eggs.

Beavers build a home in the water called a **lodge**. They chew branches from trees. Then, they carry them into a river. The opening to the lodge is under the water.

Animals also use plants to help them hide from danger. In their tree, the bird and squirrel are usually out of reach of danger. The beaver can dive into its lodge to escape.

Some animals have colors or shapes that help them hide in plants. A baby deer has light spots on its brown coat. It lies still in the tall grass. Its colors mix with the colors of the grass. The deer is very hard to see.

A **walking stick** is an insect. Its body looks like a tiny branch. If it is still, it looks like part of a plant. An animal hunting the walking stick may not see it.

Animals use plants for homes.

A. Write the word that best completes each sentence.

color	hide	homes	nest	trees

1. Many animals use plants to build their

   ______________________ .

2. Squirrels find safe homes in ______________________ .

3. A bird uses bits of wood and grass for its

   ______________________ .

4. Plants also help some animals ______________________ from danger.

5. An animal's ______________________ or shape can make it hard to see.

B. Write <u>home</u> if the animal uses plants to build a home. Write <u>safe</u> if the animal uses plants to hide. Write <u>both</u> if the animal uses plants for both.

________ 1. walking stick

________ 2. bird

________ 3. beaver

________ 4. squirrel

________ 5. baby deer

C. Write one or more sentences to answer the question.

Many squirrels are gray. How does this help them hide in a tree?

____

____

____

____

LESSON 5 How Do People Use Plants and Animals?

People use plants and animals for food, clothes, and many other things. Plants and animals make our lives possible.

Much of our food comes from plants. We eat roots like carrots and beets and green leaves like lettuce. Cherries and apples are two fruits we enjoy. We make many foods from the seeds of wheat, corn, and rice. Mushrooms are decomposers that people eat.

We use animals for many kinds of food. Cows give us milk. And milk is used to make cheese and ice cream. Chickens give us eggs. Cattle, pigs, chickens, and fish give us meat.

You are probably wearing something made from a plant or an animal. Cotton cloth is made from the cotton plant. Some **dyes** that color cloth come from plants. A down jacket is stuffed with soft feathers from ducks. We take wool from sheep to make sweaters. Animal skins are used for shoes and belts.

Plants and animals make our lives better in other ways. Wood from trees is used for lumber and to make paper. We plant grass, flowers, and trees to make our homes and parks beautiful. Pets such as dogs, cats, and birds give us company and love. People also make **medicines** from plants, decomposers, and animals.

Wool from sheep

Cloth from cotton

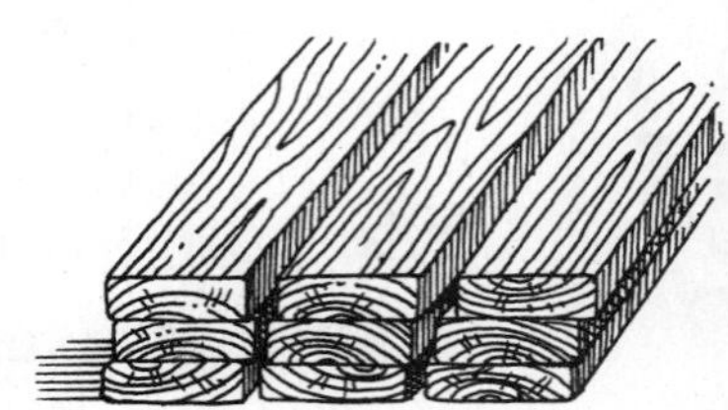

Lumber from trees

Milk from cows

Carrots and potatoes from plants

A. Write the word that best completes each sentence.

food **lettuce** **milk** **plant** **wool**

People use plants and animals for clothing and ______________________. Meat and ______________________ are foods we get from animals. Corn and ______________________ are foods we get from plants. You may be wearing cotton clothes made from part of a ______________________. Do you have a warm sweater made from ______________________? It came from a sheep.

B. Write plants, animals, or both to tell where we get each thing.

1. rice ______________________
2. carrots ______________________
3. cheese ______________________
4. paper ______________________
5. medicine ______________________
6. pets ______________________

C. Write one or more sentences to answer the question.

What are some ways life would be hard without trees?

____

____

____

LESSON 6

How Do People Help Plants and Animals?

Every living thing needs the right kind of **habitat**, or home. Some plants must grow in or near water. Some animals must have an open field or a forest for a home.

Sometimes people make life hard for plants and animals. We build in their habitats. At times, people make the water, air, or land dirty. Plants and animals living there become sick or die. People use too many plants and animals for food or clothes. This puts some plants and animals in danger. There are only a few of these plants and animals left.

Many people work to help plants and animals. People make laws to keep many kinds of living things safe. Some laws say people may not kill animals for food or any other reason. Some laws say plants must not be cut down. Laws also make people keep the air, water, and land clean.

People also set aside special places for plants and animals to live. In some city parks where people play, plants and animals can live safely. Much larger areas of land and water are saved to make habitats for plants and animals. People enjoy visiting these quiet, open places. These places are restful and beautiful. But they also give plants and animals safe places to live, grow, and raise their young.

Plants and animals need safe places to live.

A. Write three reasons why some plants and animals need help from people.

1. ______________________________

____

2. ______________________________

____

3. ______________________________

____

B. Underline the correct word or words in each sentence.

1. When people build houses on a field, the plants and animals (are safe, must find new homes).
2. To keep plants and animals out of danger, people make (roads, laws, houses).
3. A park helps plants and animals by giving them (medicine, a safe habitat, a law).
4. One reason to set aside open spaces is to give (people, plants, animals) restful and beautiful places to visit.

C. Write one or more sentences to answer the question.

What could happen if there were no laws to stop the loss of plants and animals?

____

____

____

____

CHAPTER 4

Watch Animals Use Plants

You need:

- **markers or crayons**
- **poster board**

In this activity you will make a poster showing how an animal uses plants.

Follow these steps:

1. Find a good place to watch animals. Your teacher will help you.
2. Watch to see animals using plants. Remember that animals use plants to eat, to make homes, and for safety.
3. Make a poster showing all the ways you saw animals using plants.

Write answers to these questions.

1. What animals did you see?

___

___

___

2. What are two different ways you saw the animals using plants?

___

___

___

TEST CHAPTER 4

Darken the circle next to the correct answer.

1. To make food, a plant uses
   Ⓐ water, air, and seeds.
   Ⓑ air, water, and light.
   Ⓒ stem, leaves, and roots.
   Ⓓ light, air, and roots.

2. How do animals get energy to live and grow?
   Ⓐ They make food.
   Ⓑ They eat plants or other animals.
   Ⓒ They lie in the sun.
   Ⓓ They become food for other animals.

3. Plants and animals are links, or parts, in
   Ⓐ a food chain.
   Ⓑ a food link.
   Ⓒ an animal-eater.
   Ⓓ a plant-eater.

4. Living things that break down dead plants and animals are called
   Ⓐ energy-users.
   Ⓑ decomposers.
   Ⓒ plant-eaters.
   Ⓓ animal-eaters.

5. Two kinds of decomposers are
   Ⓐ green plants and deer.
   Ⓑ grass and birds.
   Ⓒ worms and mushrooms.
   Ⓓ rabbits and hawks.

6. Why can't we see some animals hiding in plants?
   Ⓐ They look like the plants.
   Ⓑ They can disappear.
   Ⓒ They have a different color.
   Ⓓ They are bigger.

7. Which food comes from the root of a plant?
   Ⓐ cheese
   Ⓑ wheat
   Ⓒ apples
   Ⓓ beets

8. Which list shows things we get from plants?
   Ⓐ milk, feathers, and belts
   Ⓑ corn, wood, and paper
   Ⓒ rice, wool, and cotton
   Ⓓ pets, dyes, and lettuce

9. A place where an animal or a plant lives is called its
   Ⓐ link.
   Ⓑ decomposer.
   Ⓒ habitat.
   Ⓓ food chain.

10. What are two things people make to help plants and animals?
    Ⓐ houses and fields
    Ⓑ guns and lakes
    Ⓒ laws and safe parks
    Ⓓ zoos and museums

Rocks and Soil

These rocks have straight glassy sides and sharp points. They look like someone might have made them. But that is not what happened. These rocks formed underground. In this chapter you will learn about rocks. And you'll find out how rocks like these turn into the sand and soil that living things need.

- It is a kind of matter.
- It may join with others to make new matter.
- It cannot break down into other kinds of matter.

LESSON 1

What Are Rocks?

Most of Earth is rock. You see rocks around you in many forms—from mountains to sand. But what are rocks made of?

Every rock is made of one, two, or more **minerals**. Minerals are not living. They are **natural**, which means they are not made by people. A rock is made from minerals, just as a house is built of wood, brick, and glass.

Look at a rock. What color is it? How hard is it? Is it smooth or rough? Is it heavy or light? The answers to these questions are the rock's **properties**, or what the rock is like. Properties help you tell what kind of rock it is. They can even tell when and how the rock was made.

Granite is a very hard kind of rock. It is mainly a mix of four minerals. Sometimes granite has spots of different colors. One kind of mineral gives granite pink or red spots. Another kind of mineral gives granite clear, glassy spots. Granite is hard because melted rock is squeezed tightly deep inside Earth.

Limestone is another kind of rock. It is much softer than granite. It is easy to cut. Limestone is made mostly of one mineral that is usually white or light in color. Some limestone forms from fossils of sea animals. The fossils press together to make rock.

Minerals in Rocks

Granite is made mainly of four minerals.

Some limestone is made of fossils.

A. Write True if the sentence is true. Write False if the sentence is false.

_______ 1. All rocks are made from minerals.

_______ 2. Minerals are made by people.

_______ 3. All rocks are hard and smooth.

_______ 4. Granite is made mainly of four minerals.

_______ 5. Limestone is made mostly of one mineral that is white or light in color.

B. Write the word or words that tell about each kind of rock.

formed by pressing	**hard**	**soft**
formed from melted rock	**light in color**	**spotted**

Granite	Limestone
_______________	_______________
_______________	_______________
_______________	_______________

C. Write one or more sentences to answer the question.

How could you test some rocks to see how hard they are?

____

____

____

____

____

LESSON 2

What Are Minerals?

Rocks are made of many different minerals. Each mineral is different from every other mineral in some ways.

Minerals are made of **elements**. An element is a single kind of matter. You cannot break one element down into other elements. There are only about one hundred elements. They are the building blocks of everything on Earth.

Some minerals, like iron, copper, calcium and gold, are elements. Most minerals are formed when two or more elements join. These minerals have different properties than their elements. For example, the element **chlorine** is a yellow gas. The element **sodium** is a soft metal. When chlorine and sodium join, they make glassy little pieces of the mineral called salt!

When you say salt looks like glass, you are talking about a property called **luster**. Luster is the way a mineral looks when light hits it. Some minerals shine like metal. Copper has a metal luster. Quartz, like salt, has a glassy luster. Others, like limestone, look dull.

Color is another property of minerals. Some minerals are always the same color. But many minerals may have different colors. The colors may come from small pieces of special elements found in the mineral, such as iron.

Salt

Salt is a mineral. It has a glassy luster.

Gold

Gold is both an element and a mineral. It has a metal luster.

A. Write the missing word in each sentence.

1. Minerals are made of ________________________ .
   (elements, rocks, sodium)
2. Gold is an element that is also a ________________________ .
   (gas, property, mineral)
3. Most minerals made of more than one element have
   ________________________ different from those of their elements.
   (properties, shapes, lives)
4. Salt is made of chlorine and ________________________ .
   (iron, copper, sodium)
5. The shine or dullness of a mineral is called its
   ________________________.
   (luster, color, element)
6. Two properties of minerals are ________________________
   and luster.
   (salt, color, element)

B. Circle the words that show some properties of minerals.

color copper elements in them

iron luster

C. Write one or more sentences to answer the questions.

Is everything that has properties like luster and color a mineral? Why or why not?

____

____

____

LESSON 3

How Is Soil Made?

Did you ever look closely at **soil**? Soil is made of tiny pieces of rock and dead plants and animals. How is soil made?

Earth is made of rocks. Wind, rain, and ice wear away rocks into smaller pieces. This wearing away is called **weathering**.

Imagine a huge rock with a crack in it. Rainwater fills the crack and then freezes. When water freezes and turns to ice, it **expands**, or gets bigger. The expanding ice pushes on the sides of the crack and makes it bigger. After years, the crack becomes so big that the stone splits into pieces. Rain keeps falling on the pieces and breaks them into smaller pieces. Grains of sand blown by the wind also hit the broken rock. They wear off more pieces. After thousands of years, smaller and smaller pieces of rock break down to make the main part of soil.

In time, some seeds fall into the new soil. The seeds grow. Then, insects come to live in the soil and eat the plants. Over time, the plants and animals die. Decomposers break them down. Small pieces of dead plants and animals mix with the soil. These small pieces are called **humus**. Humus is an important part of soil. It makes soil rich with things that plants need to grow well. As more humus is added to soil, more plants can grow in the soil.

How Soil Is Made

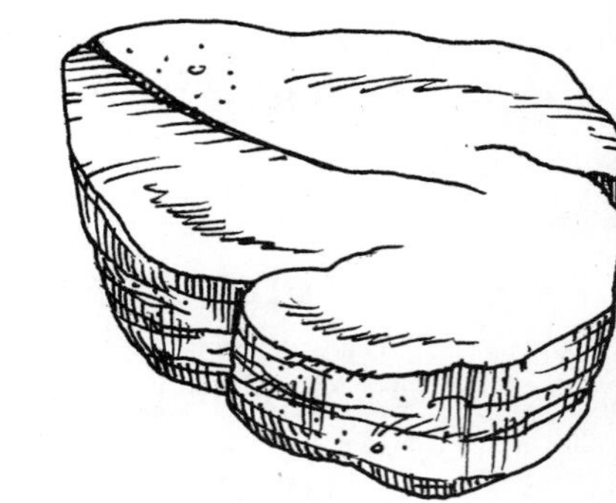

A rock splits.

A rock breaks into smaller and smaller pieces.

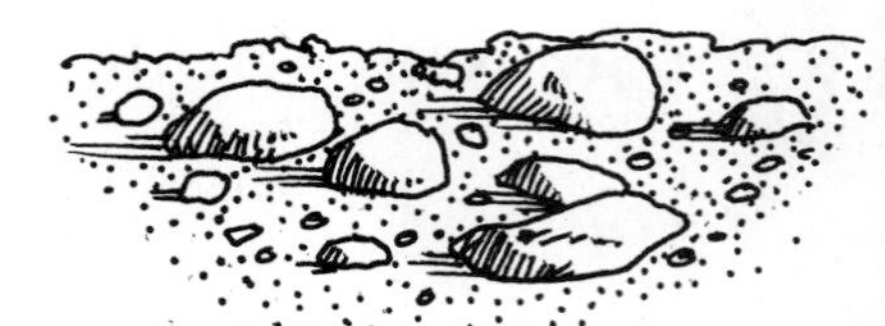

Soil forms.

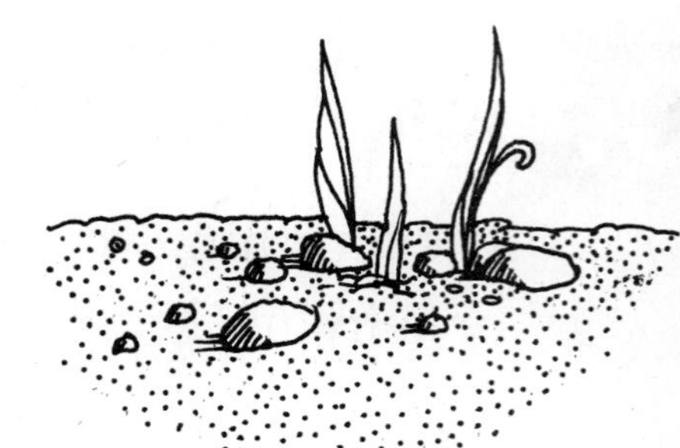

Plants begin to grow.

A. Write the word that best completes each sentence.

humus **ice** **rock** **weathering**

1. Rocks break into small pieces by ______________________ .
2. Wind, rain, and ______________________ wear away rock.
3. The main part of soil is made of tiny pieces of ______________________ .
4. Bits of broken-down dead plant and animal matter in soil are called ______________________ .

B. The sentences below tell how soil is made. Write 1, 2, 3, 4, and 5 to show the correct order. The first one is done for you.

________ Plants begin to grow in the broken pieces of rock.

____1____ Ice splits a huge rock into pieces.

________ Dead plants and animals add humus to the soil.

________ Rain and wind break rock pieces into smaller pieces.

________ Insects come to live in the plants.

C. Write one or more sentences to answer the question.

Why do you think that the breaking down of rock into smaller and smaller bits is called weathering?

____

____

____

____

LESSON 4 How Are Soils Different?

Soils are different in some important ways. For example, they are different in **texture**, in the size of their **pores**, and in color.

The pieces of rock in different soils may be different in size. The size of these pieces gives a soil its **texture**. Texture is how something feels when you touch it. Rub some soil between your fingers. If it feels bumpy and scratchy, it is probably sandy soil. The pieces of rock in sandy soil are larger than in other soils. If the soil feels soft and smooth, then the soil may be **silt**. If the soil feels slippery and sticky, it is probably **clay** soil. Clay soil has the smallest rock pieces.

Soils also have **pores**. Pores are the spaces between pieces of soil. The pores in sandy soil are larger than the pores in clay soil. You can spill sandy soil from your hands. But clay soil pieces stick together.

Pores help hold water for plants to use. If the pores are too large, like the pores in sandy soil, the soil cannot hold water. If the pores are too small, like the pores in clay soil, the water can't move through the soil easily.

Color helps show what is in soil. Humus is usually dark brown or black. Dark soils have more humus. That is good for plants. **Loam**, a dark soil with a mix of sand, silt, clay, and humus, is a good soil for plants.

Soil Textures

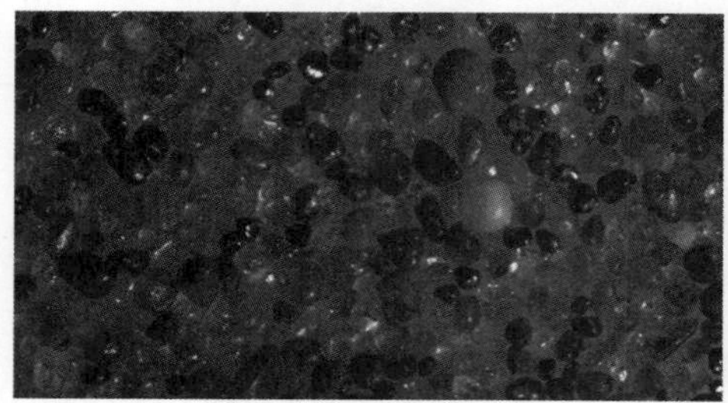

Sand has large pieces of rock.

Silt has smaller pieces of rock.

Clay has the smallest pieces of rock.

Loam

Loam is a good soil for plants.

A. Write the word or words that tell the ways soils are different.

1. ______________________________

2. ______________________________

3. ______________________________

B. Write the word or words that best complete each sentence.

humus **larger** **pores** **sandy soil** **texture** **water**

Soils have important differences. First, the size of pieces in soil gives the soil its ____________________ . Soil with the biggest pieces is called ____________________ . Second, the spaces between each piece of soil are called ____________________ . The pores in sandy soil are ____________________ than in other soils. Soil can hold ____________________ . Sandy soil does not do this well. Third, soil has color. Sandy soil is light in color, so you know it does not have much ____________________ .

C. Write one or more sentences to answer the questions.

If you were a farmer, what kind of soil would you want to have on your farm? Why?

____

____

____

____

____

LESSON 5

Why Do Plants and Animals Need Soil?

Plants, animals, and people need soil for food and homes. Why is soil so important to living things?

Most plants need soil to grow. Roots grow down into soil. Soil holds the water and minerals plants use. Plants need special minerals to live. Water carries these minerals into plants through the roots. Soil makes life possible for plants. And plants make life possible for animals and people.

Many animals eat the plants that grow in the soil. These plant eaters become food for other animals. This means all animals need plants for life. Even if an animal does not eat plants itself, it eats animals that eat plants.

Some animals, such as worms, make their homes in the soil. Worms use humus for food. They also give something back to the soil. Worms make tunnels that let in air and water. This makes the soil better for plants.

How many things have you used today that were grown in soil? The corn in your breakfast food grew in soil. The paper for this book came from trees that grew in soil. Maybe the house you live in is built from wood that came from trees. Some of the clothes you wear came from plants that grew in soil or from animals that ate plants. People, like plants and animals, need soil.

Plants, Animals, and Soil

Plants need soil, and animals need plants.

A. Write True if the sentence is true. Write False if the sentence is false.

________ **1.** Soil makes life possible for people.

________ **2.** Water and minerals from the soil move into a plant through its roots.

________ **3.** Only plant-eating animals depend on soil.

________ **4.** Worms live in soil and keep plants from growing in it.

________ **5.** People use trees for paper and wood.

B. Write the number of each sentence on the correct line.

1. Roots take in water and minerals.

2. A worm lives in soil.

3. People grow food in soil.

4. A worm makes spaces in soil.

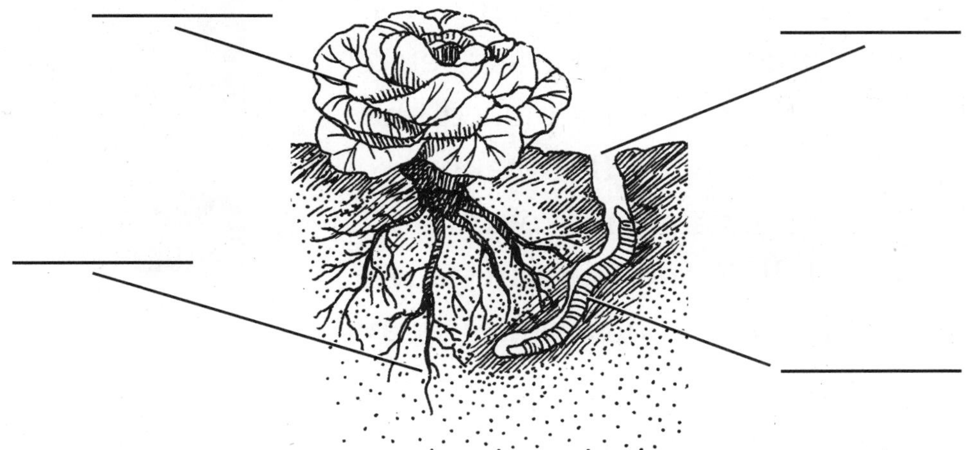

C. Write one or more sentences to answer the question.

Why do people need soil in order to have paper and furniture?

____

____

LESSON 6

How Can People Take Care of the Soil?

Soil does not stay the same. People must care for soil so that they can keep using it.

Wind and rain can blow and wash soil away. This is called **erosion**. It takes a long time to make soil, but soil can **erode**, or be carried away, quickly.

Plants hold the soil in place. When land has no plants, the soil can erode. People often cut down trees. If people leave the soil bare, it can erode.

People help stop erosion by planting. For example, they can plant new trees in place of the trees they cut down. They can plant grass, trees, and bushes in the bare soil next to roads.

Farmers have learned to slow erosion in their fields. They plant rows of grass between their crops. When the crops are picked, the grass keeps water and wind from taking soil away. On a hillside, farmers make rows of plants across the hill. Rainwater cannot run down the hill fast, so less soil washes away.

Planting the same kind of crop over and over in one field can hurt soil. The crop can take away the minerals. To keep soil healthy, farmers change what they plant in a field. Some years they may even grow grass. The grass can help make the soil healthy again.

Farmers Slow Erosion

The grass holds the soil in place when the other plants are gone.

These rows of plants run across the hill. They look a little like steps.

A. Write True if the sentence is true. Write False if the sentence is false.

_______ **1.** Wind and rain can erode soil.

_______ **2.** Bare soil does not erode.

_______ **3.** Plants help hold soil in place.

_______ **4.** Leaving strips of grass in a field slows erosion.

_______ **5.** Planting the same plants again and again makes soil healthy.

B. Put a ✔ beside each sentence that tells about something that helps soil.

_______ **1.** Wind and rain blow across bare land.

_______ **2.** People cut down trees and leave the land bare.

_______ **3.** People plant trees and bushes around a new building.

_______ **4.** A farmer plants grass between the crops.

C. Write one or more sentences to answer the questions.

In some places, heavy rains fall during the winter and spring. Little rain falls during the summer and autumn. In these places, what times of the year would more erosion happen? Why?

____

____

____

____

____

See What Is in Soil

You need:

- **newspapers**
- **hand lens**
- **large spoon**
- **plastic cup**
- **soil**
- **water**

In this activity you will find out what is in soil.

Follow these steps:

1. Put newspapers on a table. Put a small pile of soil on the newspapers.
2. Sort through the soil. Put the different kinds of soil parts into different piles. Look at the soil parts through the hand lens. Write down what you see.
3. Put two spoonfuls of soil into a cup of water. Stir the water with the spoon. Let the water sit overnight. Then, look at the water. Write down what you see.

Write answers to these questions.

1. What kinds of things make up the soil you studied?

____

____

____

2. How did the soil change overnight in the cup of water?

____

____

____

TEST CHAPTER 5

Darken the circle next to the correct answer.

1. What are all rocks made of?
   Ⓐ soil
   Ⓑ minerals
   Ⓒ granite
   Ⓓ limestone

2. The building blocks of everything on Earth are called
   Ⓐ rocks.
   Ⓑ minerals.
   Ⓒ gases.
   Ⓓ elements.

3. When you say that a mineral is dull, you are talking about its
   Ⓐ elements.
   Ⓑ metal.
   Ⓒ luster.
   Ⓓ color.

4. The wearing away of rocks by wind, rain, and ice is called
   Ⓐ weathering.
   Ⓑ expanding.
   Ⓒ freezing.
   Ⓓ splitting.

5. Pieces of dead plants and animals in the soil are called
   Ⓐ luster.
   Ⓑ properties.
   Ⓒ air.
   Ⓓ humus.

6. Which soil has the smallest pieces of rock and a sticky texture?
   Ⓐ sand
   Ⓑ silt
   Ⓒ clay
   Ⓓ loam

7. The best soil for plants to grow in is
   Ⓐ sand.
   Ⓑ silt.
   Ⓒ clay.
   Ⓓ loam.

8. Why do plants need soil?
   Ⓐ to get water and minerals
   Ⓑ to stop erosion
   Ⓒ to get air
   Ⓓ to make wood

9. What do plants do for soil?
   Ⓐ erode it
   Ⓑ make tunnels in it
   Ⓒ grow in it
   Ⓓ hold it in place

10. People help soil by slowing
    Ⓐ wind.
    Ⓑ rain.
    Ⓒ erosion.
    Ⓓ farming.

Weather

The air around Earth is changing all the time. Sometimes, it is calm. Other times, it is windy. Sometimes clouds like the ones in the picture move across the sky. They bring thunderstorms. In this chapter you will learn about the air outside and the way it changes. You'll learn how water from Earth mixes with air, makes clouds, and falls to Earth again.

What is it?

- It tells about the heat energy around it.
- It changes when heat energy is added.
- It may have liquid inside.

LESSON 1 What Is Weather?

Look outside the window. Is it hot or cold? Is it raining? Is it snowing? Is the wind blowing? You are watching the **weather**, or what the air is like outside. And the weather changes all the time.

The jungle has a wet, warm climate.

People like to know the weather where they live. They use what they know about weather to dress for school and work. They use what they know about weather to plan picnics, baseball games, and vacations. Why is the weather important to you?

People who study weather learn about air, wind, rain, and clouds. They use tools to measure. Tools measure how cool or warm the air is. They also measure how much rain falls and how fast winds blow. People watch changes in the weather. They use what they see and measure to tell you what the weather will be in the future.

The climate near the North Pole is cold all year long.

People who study weather also use what they know to tell about the **climate** in a place. The climate in a place is what the weather is like over many years. A forest, for example, can have a wet, cold climate. A jungle can have a wet, warm climate. And a desert can have a dry, hot climate. If you could visit one of these places, which climate would you like to visit?

A. Write the word or words that best complete each sentence.

air and clouds **climate** **dry** **weather** **wet**

1. What the air is like outside is the ______________________ .
2. People who study weather need to learn about ______________________ .
3. The weather in a place over many years is the ______________________ .
4. A forest can have a ______________________ , cold climate.
5. A desert can have a ______________________ , hot climate.

B. Write True if the sentence is true. Write False if the sentence is false.

________ 1. Weather can change from day to day.

________ 2. Knowing about the weather cannot help you.

________ 3. People who study weather use tools to measure how much rain falls.

________ 4. People who study weather can tell what the weather will be like tomorrow.

________ 5. A jungle can have a wet, warm climate.

C. Write one or more sentences to answer the question.

It rains in a place on one day. Then, it snows in the same place the next day. Has the climate in the place changed? Why or why not?

____

____

LESSON 2 What Is Temperature?

Rain, snow, oceans, air, and clouds in the sky are all examples of **matter**. Anything that takes up space is matter. We can't see some kinds of matter, like gases. But all gases still take up space. The gas we call air is a good example. When you blow into a balloon, the balloon gets bigger. This is because it fills with air, and air takes up space. When you let air out of a balloon, the balloon gets smaller. The air leaves the balloon and goes into the room.

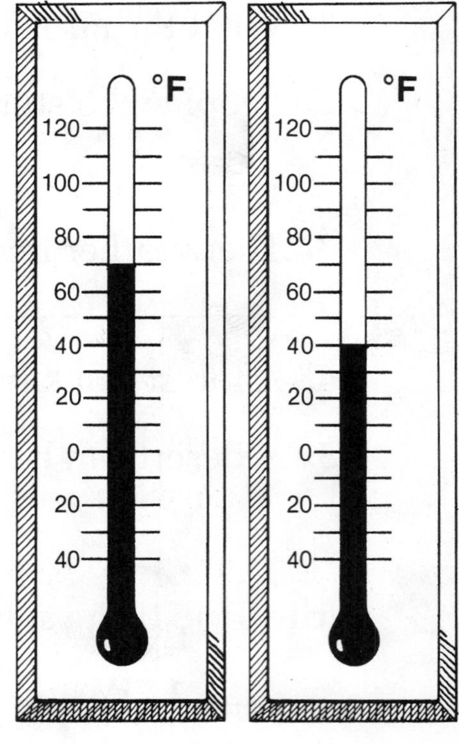

The liquid in the thermometer on the left is warmer and takes up more space inside the thermometer.

Energy comes in different forms. **Heat energy** is one kind of energy. Energy from the sun heats everything on Earth. It heats the air in the sky and the water in the ocean.

All matter has heat energy. Some matter has more heat energy than other matter. We use the word **temperature** to tell how hot matter is. When we measure the temperature of air, we learn how hot the air is. Remember, air is matter, and matter has heat energy.

You need a **thermometer** to measure the temperature of air. Some thermometers have a special liquid inside them. When heat energy is added to the liquid, the liquid grows bigger. It uses more space inside the thermometer. We read the numbers on the outside of the thermometer to know how much heat energy is in the air.

A. Write <u>True</u> if the sentence is true. Write <u>False</u> if the sentence is false.

_______ **1.** All matter takes up space.

_______ **2.** Air is a kind of matter.

_______ **3.** Heat energy is one kind of energy.

_______ **4.** Adding heat energy to matter does not change the matter's temperature.

B. Write the missing word or words in each sentence.

1. Air, clouds, oceans, and snow all take up space and are examples of _______________ .
(energy, matter, heat energy)

2. All matter has heat _______________ .
(temperature, energy, space)

3. Energy from _______________ heats everything on Earth.
(matter, the sun, weather)

4. The more heat energy matter has, the higher its _______________ is.
(thermometer, temperature, energy)

5. Temperature can be measured using a _______________ .
(gas, balloon, thermometer)

C. Write one or more sentences to answer the question.

Could you add heat energy to water in a cup just by taking the cup outside? Explain.

____

____

____

LESSON 3

What Are Air and Wind?

Air is all around us. Layers of air cover Earth. Air pushes out in all directions. You can see the **force**, or push, of air. Gently push your finger into a balloon filled with air. Then, remove your finger. The air in the balloon pushes back.

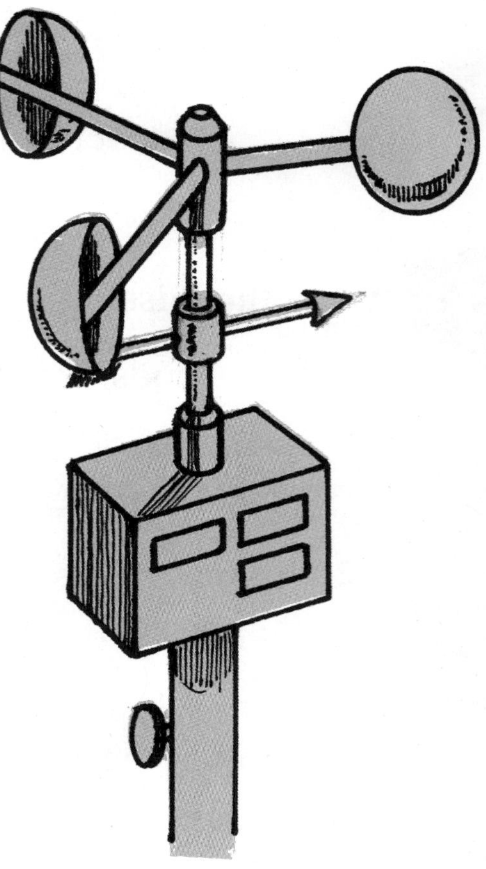

The top part of the anemometer turns to measure wind speed. The arrow is a weather vane. It points in the direction from which the wind blows.

There is another way that you can use a balloon to see the force of air. You already know what happens when you blow too much air into a balloon. The balloon pops. The force of the air breaks the balloon. This force of air is called **air pressure**.

Cold air and warm air have different air pressures. Cold air has high pressure. Warm air has low pressure. When cold air pushes warm air, **wind** forms. Wind is air that moves. When there is only a little difference in air pressure, the wind is gentle. When there is a lot of difference in air pressure, the wind is strong.

People who study weather use special tools to learn about air and wind. You already know that they use a thermometer to measure the temperature of air. Did you know that they can use a **weather vane** to measure the direction from which the wind is blowing? And they can use an **anemometer** to measure how fast the wind blows.

A. Write the word or words that best complete each sentence.

1. Earth is covered by layers of ____________________ .
   (climate, air, energy)

2. The push, or force, of air is called ____________________ .
   (matter, air pressure, wind)

3. When cold air pushes warm air, ____________________ forms.
   (fog, heat, wind)

4. The direction from which the wind blows is measured with a
   ____________________ .
   (weather vane, anemometer, thermometer)

5. Wind speed is measured with ____________________ .
   (a weather vane, an anemometer, a thermometer)

B. Put a ✔ next to the tools people use to learn about weather.

_______ 1. temperature

_______ 2. thermometer

_______ 3. air pressure

_______ 4. wind

_______ 5. weather vane

_______ 6. anemometer

C. Write one or more sentences to answer the question.

On one day, there is almost no wind. On the next day, it is windy.
How did the weather change?

____

____

LESSON 4

What Is the Water Cycle?

When a puddle dries, the water is not lost forever. The water has become part of a big circle called the **water cycle**. Water changes its form in the water cycle, but it never disappears.

One part of the water cycle that you can see is **rain**. After it rains, everything is wet—the grass, the sidewalks, and the streets. Some of this rain sinks deep into the ground. And some of the rain spills into ponds, streams, and rivers.

Soon, the sun shines again. Heat from the sun **evaporates**, or dries, the rain. When rain evaporates, the liquid water changes form. It becomes a gas you cannot see. This gas is called **water vapor**. The sun is always evaporating water from puddles, ponds, lakes, streams, rivers, and oceans.

Water vapor is light, not heavy. It rises into the sky. When there is enough water vapor in the sky, the water vapor **condenses**, or gathers together. Water vapor that condenses isn't a gas anymore. It is liquid water again. We see the liquid water as a cloud.

Liquid water is heavy. When it falls, we call it rain. If the air is cold, the water may fall as snow or ice. The rain, snow, or ice falls to the ground. The sun melts the snow and ice. The liquid water evaporates again, returning to the water cycle.

The Water Cycle

Water keeps moving through the water cycle.

A. Write the word or words that best complete each sentence.

clouds **rain** **water cycle** **water vapor**

1. Water changes to vapor and back to water again as part of the ______________________ .
2. When the sun evaporates water, the water turns into ______________________ .
3. Water vapor condenses into ______________________ in the sky.
4. Water may fall from clouds as ______________________ , snow, or ice.

B. Write the correct name for each part of the water cycle.

Clouds

Rain

Water vapor

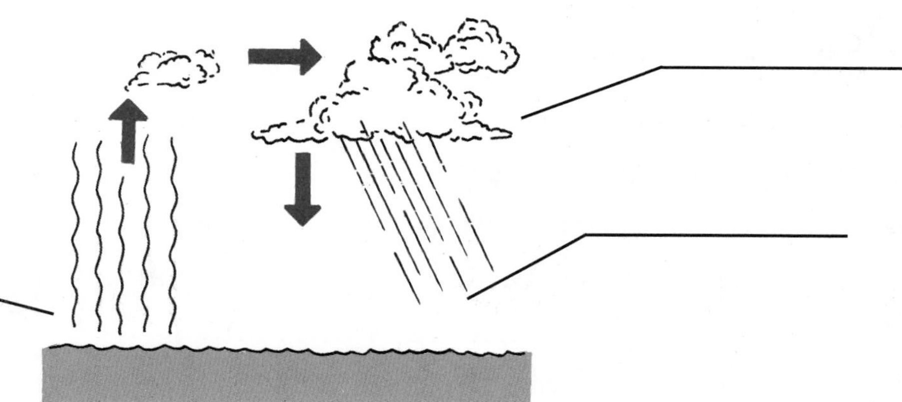

C. Write one or more sentences to answer the question.

Are the black clouds you see before a thunderstorm heavy or light? Explain your answer.

____

____

____

LESSON 5

What Are Clouds?

Imagine looking out your window. It is the middle of the day, but the sky looks dark. Lightning zips through the air. A loud crash follows. You hear thunder. The sky is filled with huge, dark clouds. Rain pours down. It is another summer storm.

You know that the clouds you see are part of the water cycle. But not all clouds look the same. Some are so thin you can see through them. Others look like big, white pillows. Each kind of cloud has its own name. **Cirrus clouds** form high in the sky. They are thin and look like feathers. The drops of water that make cirrus clouds freeze into tiny pieces of ice.

Cumulus clouds are another kind of cloud. They look like heaps of white cotton balls. The huge, dark clouds that bring storms are **cumulonimbus clouds**. These clouds can be very tall or thick. Rain, lightning, and thunder can come from these clouds.

Stratus clouds look like flat, white sheets. They float near the ground. Sometimes, stratus clouds hide the tops of mountains or very tall buildings. **Fog** is a kind of stratus cloud. Fog begins close to the ground. Then, it rises into the air. What do you feel when you walk through fog? You feel wet. That is because all clouds are made of drops of water.

Clouds

A. Write the word that best completes each sentence.

cirrus **drops** **fog** **stratus**

1. Clouds that look thin and feathery and are high in the sky are called ________________ clouds.
2. The tops of mountains are sometimes hidden by ________________ clouds.
3. The cloud that begins close to the ground is ________________ .
4. Clouds are made of ________________ of water.

B. Draw a line from each kind of cloud to the words that describe it.

1. cirrus	huge and dark
2. cumulus	look like big, white cotton balls
3. cumulonimbus	high in the sky and look thin and feathery
4. stratus	flat sheets that float near the ground

C. Write one or more sentences to answer the question.

Why do you think cumulonimbus clouds are so dark?

____

____

____

____

____

LESSON 6 How Do People Change the Air?

You breathe air. You fly kites in the air. You use air to fill balloons and the tires on your bike. We use the air, and sometimes, we change the air. When we drive our cars or run our factories, we put dirt and gases into the air. Dirt and gases that we put in air are called **air pollution**.

Cars and trucks cause air pollution.

Imagine a busy city filled with cars, trucks, and factories. Fog hides the tops of the buildings. Dirt and gases enter the air and mix with the fog. The air changes color. Breathing the air makes some people sick. This kind of air pollution is called **smog**.

Some scientists think that air pollution traps too much heat. The heat stays close to Earth, warming the air, land, and oceans. This warming is called **global warming**. Scientists worry that in time the heat will change Earth's climates. Ice near the poles may melt. Oceans may rise. Ocean water might cover the towns and cities we build near ocean shores.

Factories can also cause air pollution.

What are some things you can do to help keep air clean? You already know that cars, buses, and trucks make lots of air pollution. Maybe the next time you want to go somewhere, you could ride your bike. Or you could share a ride with your friends. You can do something to make less air pollution.

A. Underline the correct word or words in each sentence.

1. Factories and (cars, bikes, oceans) pollute the air.
2. Air pollution can make people (breathe, fly kites, sick).
3. Some scientists think air pollution can make Earth (colder, wetter, warmer).

B. Write the word or words that best complete each sentence.

air pollution **bike** **global warming** **water** **smog**

1. The dirt and gases that come from cars and factories are called ______________________.
2. When the pollution from cars mixes with fog in the air, ______________________ forms.
3. Scientists think that air pollution might cause ______________________ and raise temperatures on Earth.
4. If ice near the poles melt, ocean ______________________ may cover some towns and cities.
5. One way to make less air pollution is to ride a ______________________ instead of driving a car.

C. Write one or more sentences to answer the question.

How could global warming affect the climate where you live?

____

____

CHAPTER 6

Make a Cloud

You need:

- plastic bottle with the top cut off
- cup of hot water
- tape
- plastic wrap
- 5 ice cubes

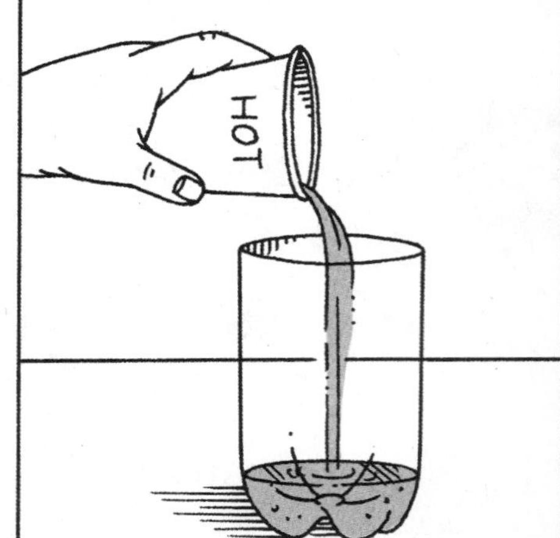

In this activity you will model a cloud.

Follow these steps:

1. Very carefully pour the cup of hot water into the bottle.
2. Cover the opening at the top of the bottle with the plastic wrap. Tape the plastic to the sides of the bottle.
3. Place 5 ice cubes on top of the plastic wrap. Then, watch the inside of the bottle.

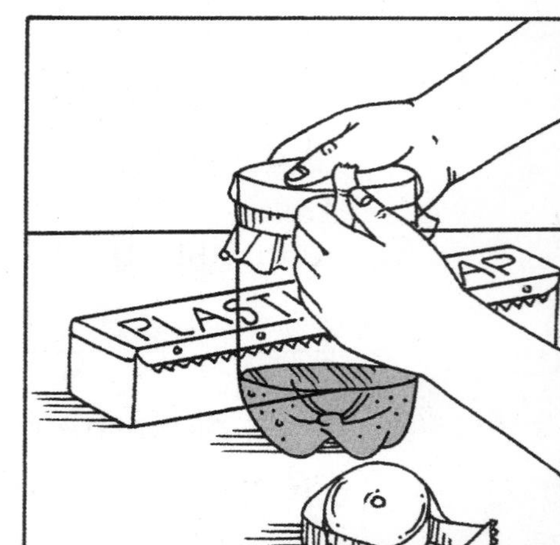

Write sentences to answer these questions.

1. What did you see under the plastic wrap?

 ____

2. What happened to the hot water in the bottle?

 ____

3. What happened to the water vapor in the bottle?

 ____

 ____

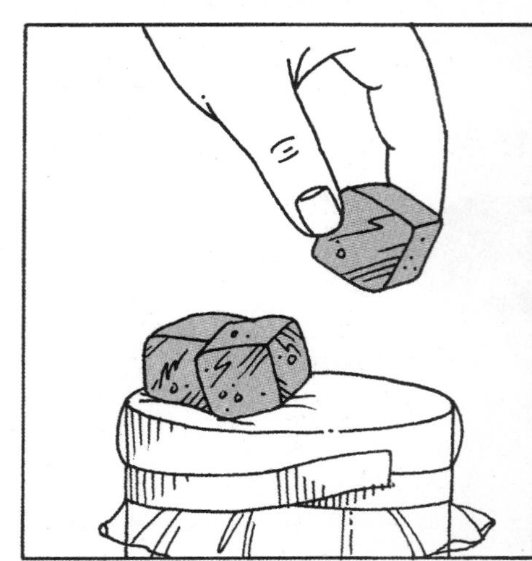

Darken the circle next to the correct answer.

1. Rain, sunshine, clouds, and temperatures are all parts of
Ⓐ air pressure.
Ⓑ air pollution.
Ⓒ global warming.
Ⓓ weather.

2. The weather of a place over many years is called its
Ⓐ temperature.
Ⓑ air pressure.
Ⓒ climate.
Ⓓ pollution.

3. What does all matter have?
Ⓐ cold energy
Ⓑ heat energy
Ⓒ air pressure
Ⓓ wind pressure

4. A thermometer measures
Ⓐ wind speed.
Ⓑ air pressure.
Ⓒ temperature.
Ⓓ wind direction.

5. The push, or force, of air is called
Ⓐ temperature.
Ⓑ climate.
Ⓒ wind.
Ⓓ air pressure.

6. What is wind?
Ⓐ moving air
Ⓑ evaporating water
Ⓒ drops of water
Ⓓ clouds

7. Water keeps changing its form as it moves through the
Ⓐ water vapor.
Ⓑ air pollution.
Ⓒ air pressure.
Ⓓ water cycle.

8. What does the sun do to rainwater?
Ⓐ condenses it
Ⓑ freezes it
Ⓒ evaporates it
Ⓓ melts it

9. Clouds are made of
Ⓐ moving air.
Ⓑ drops of water.
Ⓒ high-pressure air.
Ⓓ strong winds.

10. What causes air pollution?
Ⓐ dirt and gases from cars and factories
Ⓑ global warming
Ⓒ bicycles
Ⓓ melting icebergs

Careers

Farmer

A farmer grows grains, fruits, and vegetables. Farmers also raise animals, such as cows, pigs, and chickens. Without farmers, you would not have food to eat or clothes to wear. Most farmers sell what they grow and raise to other people.

Farmers do different farm work at different times of the year. For example, farmers plant corn seeds in the spring. In the fall, the farmers gather the corn from their plants.

Air Quality Technician

To keep healthy, people need to breathe clean air. Clean air is air that does not have dirt and smoke in it. An air quality technician helps make sure the air is clean.

Air quality technicians measure how much dirt and smoke there is in the air. They also find out where the dirt is coming from.

Jeweler

A jeweler makes rings, necklaces, bracelets, and earrings, which are called jewelry. Jewelers fix jewelry, too. Some jewelers cut minerals called gemstones into beautiful shapes. They shine the gemstones and use them to make jewelry. Jewelers do many things by hand but sometimes use machines to help them do their work.

Unit 3

Physical Science

This power plant makes the energy that runs its own lights and other lights for miles around. People also use energy to heat buildings and homes, to cook their food, and to run computers and televisions. In this unit you will learn how people use materials around them to make energy. You will also learn how people use materials to build homes, schools, and other buildings.

Matter and Energy

Every day people throw away trash. But some people recycle the things they use. That means that they return things that can be made into new things and used again. The recycled things are sent to a recycling center. Workers, like the one in this picture, divide the recycled materials into groups. In this chapter you will learn more about recycling and about other ways to reuse materials.

- People take it from the ground.
- It is burned for energy.
- In time, it will be gone.

Where Do People Live?

When you go camping, you probably sleep in a tent. The tent keeps you dry in the rain. It keeps you warm in the cool air. The tent is your **shelter**. The tent keeps you comfortable so you can enjoy your camping trip.

Rain and snow slide off the roofs of these houses.

People have always needed shelter. Some people in the world still live in tents. But many people live in houses and tall buildings. Houses keep people dry in the rain. They keep people warm in the winter and cool in the summer.

Houses have many shapes and sizes. Some houses are square. Others are round. Some stand on tall poles above the ground. Some even float on water.

These houses will not be flooded when heavy rains come.

Some houses have flat roofs. These roofs help people stay cool. Some houses have steep roofs. Rain and snow slide off these roofs. Some roofs are made of grass and mud. Other roofs are made of hard clay or even metal. Some houses have walls of mud. Others have walls of stone or wood.

The materials people use to build houses come from the places where they live. These materials are called **natural resources**. Grass, mud, stones, and trees are natural resources. In very cold places, ice is a natural resource. Some people use the ice to build houses. Do you know what we call these houses?

A. Write True if the sentence is true. Write False if the sentence is false.

_______ 1. A tent is not a shelter.

_______ 2. People have always needed shelter.

_______ 3. Houses keep people dry in wet weather.

_______ 4. All houses have flat roofs.

_______ 5. Materials people use to build their houses come from the places where they live.

B. Write the word or words that best complete each sentence.

natural resources **mud** **shapes and sizes** **steep**

1. Houses can be built in many different

   _______________ .

2. Rain and snow slide off roofs that are

   _______________ .

3. People in some parts of the world build walls of

   _______________ .

4. Grass, mud, stones, and trees are _______________ .

C. Write one or more sentences to answer the question.

In crowded places there are usually more apartment buildings than houses. Why?

____

____

LESSON 2 How Do People Choose Building Materials?

Imagine you live where it is warm all year. Gentle rains fall almost every day. There are many trees that have huge leaves. The leaves are easy to cut and shape. If you were going to build a house in this place, what natural resources would you use? What shape would your house have?

People use the wood from trees to build homes.

When people build houses, they must know something about their climate. They must also know what kinds of natural resources work best in their climate.

In some places, the weather is warm and wet. People build houses from mud and grass to keep cool and dry. In other places, the weather is cold and snowy. People build houses from stone and wood to keep warm and dry.

This house is made of bamboo and grass. It is perfect for a hot climate.

Some materials, like mud, large leaves, and wood, are easy to use as building materials. For example, clay or mud is easy to shape into **bricks**. Stone and metals are hard to cut and shape. But people use these resources to build their houses, too.

Where you live, your house may be made of many different natural resources. You may have walls made of bricks. You may have doors made of wood and a roof made of metal. Even the windows in your house are made from material found in sand.

This house is made of many different materials, such as brick, wood, metal, and glass.

A. Write True if the sentence is true. Write False if the sentence is false.

________ **1.** A house made of leaves keeps out cold weather.

________ **2.** People need to know about their climate before they build a house.

________ **3.** Some people build houses from mud and grass to keep cool and dry.

________ **4.** People can use different materials to build one house.

B. Write the word or words that best complete each sentence.

1. People need to know what kinds of ____________________ work well in their climate.
(shapes, bricks, natural resources)

2. Houses made of stone and wood keep people ____________________ in cold weather.
(cool, warm, wet)

3. It is easy to shape ____________________ into bricks.
(clay, leaves, stone)

4. It is hard to cut and shape ____________________ .
(metals, leaves, clay)

C. Write one or more sentences to answer the question.

What materials might people who live near a forest use to build houses?

____

____

____

____

How Do People Use Energy in Buildings?

You already know that energy lets us do work. We use energy in our homes to stay cool in the summer and warm in the winter. We use energy to watch television and to cook our dinner. And we use energy to make light so we can see in the dark.

This mixer uses electricity.

Many people use a kind of energy called **electricity**. A **power plant** makes electricity for a town or city. Some power plants use running water to make electricity. Others use **fossil fuels**, such as **oil**, **coal**, and **natural gas**. These fuels were made underground from the dead parts of plants and animals that lived long ago.

This furnace sends heat all through the house.

Electricity made at the power plant goes to your home through special lines, or **wires**. More wires run through the walls of your house. Things that use electricity, such as your television, have wires that go into special places in the walls.

Electricity is one kind of energy people use in their homes. Some people also have a special machine called a **furnace**. Most furnaces change fossil fuels into heat energy. The energy warms the air and water in the house.

What kinds of things in your home need energy to work? Where is the power plant where you live?

A. Write True if the sentence is true. Write False if the sentence is false.

_______ 1. Many things around the house, such as televisions and stoves, need energy to work.

_______ 2. Electricity is a kind of energy.

_______ 3. Some power plants use oil and natural gas.

_______ 4. Fossil fuels come from the air.

_______ 5. Electricity flows through special lines called pipes.

_______ 6. A furnace changes heat energy into fossil fuels.

B. Draw a line to complete each sentence.

1. Fossil fuels	warms the air in a house.
2. Electricity	makes electricity for a town or city.
3. Heat energy	come from under the ground.
4. A power plant	can flow through wires.

C. Write one or more sentences to answer the question.

Coal is a fossil fuel. How do you think we get coal from the ground?

____

____

____

____

____

Do We Have Enough Natural Resources?

You know that people use the natural resources they find in the places where they live. Trees, clay, grass, and fossil fuels are some natural resources. Look around you. What other natural resources do you see?

To help save forests, people plant new trees.

Each year, more people use more natural resources. Some people worry that we are using too many natural resources too fast. They are afraid we will use up all our natural resources.

Some people work to find ways to keep our natural resources safe. For example, some companies cut down trees to sell the wood. Then, they plant new trees. The trees grow to make new forests.

You can work to save natural resources, too. Remember what you learned about electricity. To make electricity, power plants must use natural resources. How could you help save these resources? You could use less electricity. When you **reduce**, or use less electricity, you save natural resources.

There are also other ways you can save natural resources. You can **reuse** things, or use them over and over again. Or you can **recycle** old things. When you recycle, you return things you used, so they can be made into new things. When you reduce, reuse, or recycle, you help save natural resources.

A. Put a ✔ next to the natural resources.

________ 1. trees

________ 2. clay

________ 3. houses

________ 4. electricity

________ 5. grass

________ 6. oil

________ 7. coal

B. Write the missing word in each sentence.

1. People are starting to worry that natural ____________________ will run out.
(electricity, resources, shelters)

2. You can use less ____________________ in your home by turning off lights.
(electricity, coal, oil)

3. When you use things over and over again, you ____________________ them.
(reduce, reuse, recycle)

4. When you return things to be made into new things, you ____________________ them.
(reduce, reuse, recycle)

C. Write one or more sentences to answer the question.

Some people put plastic over windows to keep cold air from blowing into their homes. How does this save energy?

____

____

____

____

LESSON 5 What Other Kinds of Building Materials Will We Use in the Future?

When we throw something away, where does it go? People who want to save natural resources reuse and recycle the things we throw away. For example, did you know that we throw away millions of rubber tires each year? What kinds of things do you throw away?

These old tires can be recycled to make building materials.

People can recycle tiny pieces of rubber tires to make many things. The recycled rubber is chopped into tiny pieces and put into walls. It is made into floors. And rubber is even shaped into furniture to use inside the house.

When some people build houses, they use recycled or reused materials. They make bricks from glass from empty bottles and old car windows. The glass is broken into fine pieces and then melted to shape the bricks. People press the dead parts of plants, such as wheat and oats, into big blocks. They use the blocks to build walls. To cover the walls, people make boards from beans. They mix dust from rocks with glue to make floors, and recycled plastic milk bottles to make carpets.

People want to be cool in the summer and warm in the winter. So they put materials inside the walls of their homes to make the walls thick. Some people use torn newspapers and pieces of material from T-shirts and pants.

A. Write True if the sentence is true. Write False if the sentence is false.

_______ 1. People who want to save natural resources throw away rubber, bottles, and cans.

_______ 2. The only material that cannot be recycled is rubber.

_______ 3. People can mix dust from rocks with glue to make floors.

_______ 4. Material inside the walls of houses can help keep people warm in the winter.

B. Write the word or words that best complete each sentence.

glass milk bottles rubber walls

1. Walls for houses can be made of recycled _______________ .
2. Bricks can be made from recycled _______________ .
3. Plants such as wheat, oats, and beans can also be used to make _______________ .
4. People can make carpets from recycled _______________ .

C. Write one or more sentences to answer the question.

One good reason to recycle is to help save natural resources. What do you think is another reason?

____

____

____

LESSON 6 What Other Kinds of Energy Will We Use in the Future?

You need energy to make things work. You learned that fossil fuels are often used to make that energy. But fossil fuels are natural resources. In time, they will be gone. Then, we will need new ways to make energy.

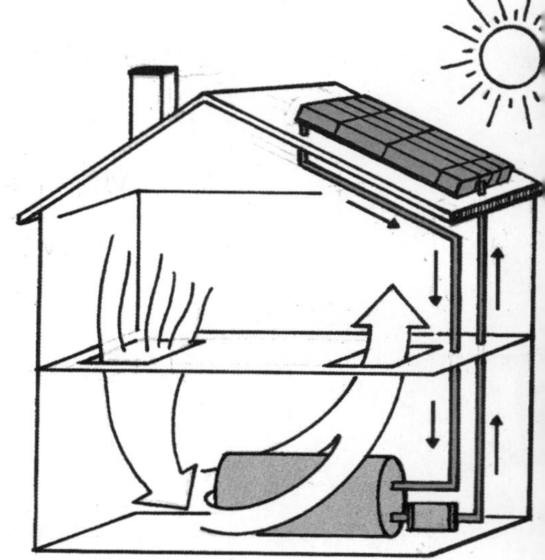

This house uses solar energy for heat.

One natural resource that will last for millions and millions of years is the sun. Energy from the sun, called **solar energy**, can be turned into energy for our homes.

Wind is another natural resource that will always be available. **Windmills** have arms that turn in the wind. When the arms turn, the windmill changes wind energy into electrical energy. Windmills are built in special places that have lots of wind. When many windmills are built in the same place, we call that place a windmill farm.

These windmills are changing wind power into electricity.

Another natural resource that will last a long time is **magma**, hot melted rock found inside Earth. In some places, magma comes close to Earth's surface. We take heat energy from Earth's magma, and change it into energy for our homes. This kind of energy is called **geothermal energy**.

So in the future, your home may use a new kind of energy to make electricity. Perhaps it will be solar energy, wind energy, or geothermal energy. Which kind of energy would work best where you live?

A. Write the missing word or words in each sentence.

1. Fossil fuels are natural resources that will

   ______________________ .

   (run out, last forever, become magma)

2. A natural resource that will last for millions of years is

   ______________________ .

   (oil, the sun, coal)

3. Windmills can turn wind energy into ______________________ energy.

   (electrical, fossil fuel, solar)

4. Many windmills in one place is called a

   ______________________ .

   (solar farm, windmill farm, magma farm)

5. Geothermal energy comes from Earth's

   ______________________ .

   (wind, fossil fuels, magma)

B. Draw a line to complete each sentence.

1. Solar energy	comes from deep inside Earth.
2. Windmills	comes from the sun.
3. Geothermal energy	change energy from the wind.

C. Write one or more sentences to answer the question.

How might weather affect a house that uses solar energy?

____

____

____

CHAPTER 7

Build a Model House

You need:

- **clay**
- **wood sticks**
- **construction paper**
- **scissors**
- **tape**
- **other art materials**

In this activity you will build a model house that uses natural resources found in your area.

Follow these steps:

1. What natural resources do you have in your area? Do you have a lot of trees or stones? Find natural resources, such as stones and fallen twigs, that can be used as building materials.
2. Make a model house for your area. Keep your climate in mind as you build.
3. Test your model house. If it snows a lot in your area, put weights on the roof to model snow. If it rains a lot, drizzle water over the roof to see if the house stays dry.

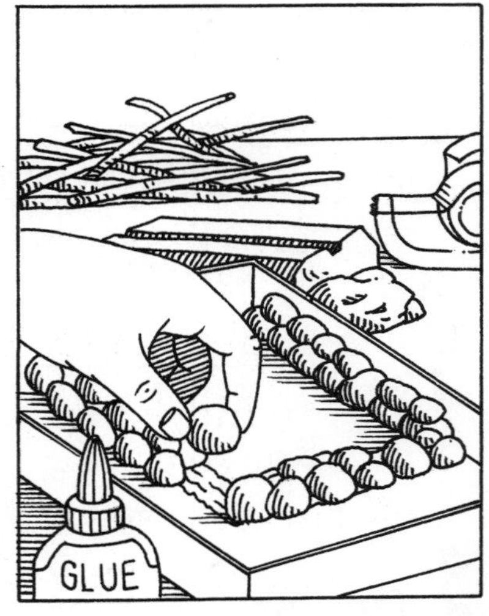

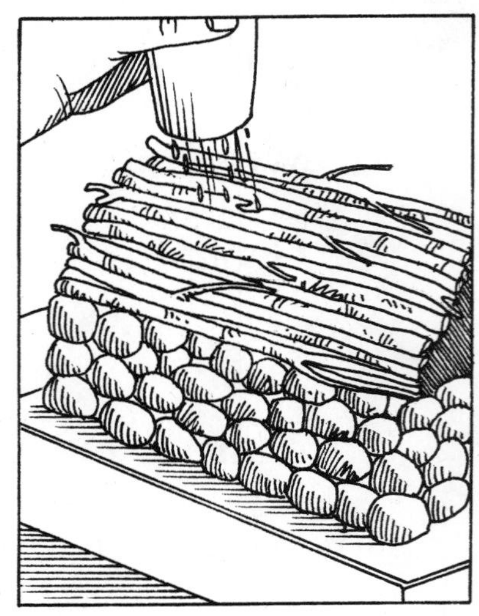

Write sentences to answer these questions.

1. What natural resources did you use for your house?

2. Would your house work well in your climate? Why or why not?

TEST CHAPTER 7

Darken the circle next to the correct answer.

1. What have people always needed for protection from the weather?
   Ⓐ coal
   Ⓑ energy
   Ⓒ bricks
   Ⓓ shelter

2. Building materials are made from
   Ⓐ solar energy.
   Ⓑ wind energy.
   Ⓒ only wood and stones.
   Ⓓ natural resources.

3. Electricity is a form of
   Ⓐ fossil fuel.
   Ⓑ heat.
   Ⓒ energy.
   Ⓓ building material.

4. Where do fossil fuels come from?
   Ⓐ under the ground
   Ⓑ the wind
   Ⓒ wires
   Ⓓ bamboo

5. What is one way to save natural resources?
   Ⓐ use less electricity
   Ⓑ cut down more trees
   Ⓒ throw away old materials
   Ⓓ use more hot water

6. When you use things over and over again, you
   Ⓐ reduce.
   Ⓑ reuse.
   Ⓒ recycle.
   Ⓓ rewind.

7. What can people put in walls to keep their homes cool in the summer?
   Ⓐ magma
   Ⓑ coal
   Ⓒ torn newspapers
   Ⓓ glass bottles

8. Solar energy comes from
   Ⓐ the sun.
   Ⓑ the ocean.
   Ⓒ the wind.
   Ⓓ under the ground.

9. Windmills change wind energy into
   Ⓐ solar energy.
   Ⓑ geothermal energy.
   Ⓒ electrical energy.
   Ⓓ fossil fuel energy.

10. Geothermal energy comes from
    Ⓐ the sun.
    Ⓑ the ocean.
    Ⓒ the wind.
    Ⓓ inside Earth.

Building Inspector

A building inspector looks at buildings while they are being built. Building inspectors check to make sure the buildings will be safe. They also check the safety of houses, schools, hospitals, and other buildings.

Building inspectors look at every part of a building. They look at the walls to see if they are strong enough to hold up the building. Some inspectors look at the pipes that carry water. Others check wires that carry power.

Electrician

An electrician works with things that use or run by electricity. Without electricians, lights, computers, and televisions would not work. Electricians put wires in the walls of a building when it is being built. The wires carry power to things like lights and computers.

Electricians also repair things that have stopped working. If a house is not getting any power, an electrician might have to repair the wires in the walls.

Environmental Architect

An environmental architect plans buildings that won't hurt the land or its plants or animals. Environmental architects may plan buildings that use the sun or wind for power. In these buildings, they try to use as many recycled materials as they can.

Glossary

A

acorn, page 8.
An acorn has the seed of an oak tree inside it.

adults, page 8.
Plants that are able to make new seeds are adults. Adult plants and animals are able to reproduce.

air pollution, page 100.
Air pollution includes dirt and gases that people put in the air.

air pressure, page 94.
Air pressure is the force with which air pushes on something.

amphibian, page 32.
An amphibian is an animal, like a frog, that lives both in water and on dry land.

anemometer, page 94.
An anemometer measures how fast the wind is blowing.

animal-eaters, page 60.
Animal-eaters are animals that use other animals for food.

B

ball and socket joints, page 42.
Ball and socket joints allow one bone to be moved in a circle while another stays still. Shoulders are ball and socket joints.

blood, page 46.
Blood travels all around the body. It carries food and air to all parts of the body. Then it returns to the heart.

bone marrow, page 40.
Bone marrow is the soft inside part of a bone.

bones, page 40.
Bones are parts inside the human body. Bones are hard on the outside and soft on the inside.

bricks, page 110.
Bricks are building materials made from clay or mud.

C

calcium, page 48.
Calcium makes bones hard and strong.

cartilage, page 40.
Cartilage is a tough material inside the human body. The outside parts of the ears are made of cartilage.

caterpillar, page 30.
A caterpillar is a butterfly larva, which is the part of a butterfly's life cycle between the egg and the pupa.

chlorine, page 76.
The element chlorine is a yellow gas.

cirrus clouds, page 98.
Cirrus clouds form high in the sky. They are thin and look like feathers.

clay, page 80.
Clay is soil that feels slippery and sticky.

climate, page 90.
The climate in a place is what the weather is like over many years.

coal, page 112.
Coal is a kind of fossil fuel.

condenses, page 96.
When water vapor, which is a gas, condenses, it becomes liquid water.

cumulonimbus clouds, page 98.
Cumulonimbus clouds are the huge, dark clouds that bring storms. These clouds can be very tall or thick. Rain, lightning, and thunder can come from these clouds.

cumulus clouds, page 98.
Cumulus clouds look like heaps of white cotton balls.

D

decomposers, page 62.
Decomposers are special living things that use dead plants and animals for food.

dyes, page 66.
Dyes are used to color cloth. Some dyes come from plants.

E

electricity, page 112.
Electricity is one kind of energy people use in their homes. Things like televisions run on electricity.

element, page 76.
An element is a single kind of matter. You cannot break one element down into other elements.

energy, pages 50 and 92.
Energy is power the body gets from food. Energy also comes in different forms. Heat energy is one kind of energy.

erode, page 84.
Wind and rain erode, or carry, soil away.

erosion, page 84.
Erosion happens when wind and rain blow and wash soil away.

evaporates, page 96.
When liquid water evaporates, it becomes a gas called water vapor.

expands, page 78.
When something expands, it gets bigger and takes up more space. When water freezes and turns to ice, it expands.

F

fixed joints, page 42.
Fixed joints hold bones in place with no movement. They are found in the skull.

fog, page 98.
Fog is a kind of stratus cloud. Fog begins close to the ground. Then it rises into the air.

food chain, page 60.
A food chain is formed by the living things that use each other for food. For example, grass is eaten by a cricket, the cricket is eaten by a frog, and the frog is eaten by a hawk.

food pyramid, page 50.
The food pyramid shows the kinds of foods you should eat most often and those foods you should eat the least.

force, page 94.
Force is a push or pull.

fossil fuels, page 112.
Fossil fuels, such as oil, coal, and natural gas, were made from dead plants and animals that lived long ago. We take fossil fuels from under the ground.

furnace, page 112.
A furnace is a special machine that changes fossil fuels into heat energy. The energy warms the air and water in a house.

G

geothermal energy, page 118.
Geothermal energy is heat energy that comes from deep inside Earth.

global warming, page 100.
Global warming is caused when air pollution traps heat that stays close to Earth, warming the air, land, and oceans.

granite, page 74.
Granite is a very hard kind of rock.

H

habitat, page 68.
A living thing's habitat is where it lives.

heart, page 46.
The heart is made of the strongest muscles in the body. It makes blood move to all parts of the body.

heartbeat, page 46.
A heartbeat happens each time the muscles in the heart squeeze together.

heat energy, page 92.
Heat energy is one kind of energy. Energy from the sun heats everything on Earth. All matter has heat energy.

hinge joints, page 42.
Hinge joints let bones move back and forth. Knees and elbows are hinge joints.

humus, page 78.
Humus is small pieces of dead plants and animals that mix with soil.

J

joints, page 42.
Joints are places where bones meet.

L

larva, page 30.
The larva is the part of a butterfly's life cycle between the egg and the pupa. The larva is also called a caterpillar.

life cycle, page 8.
A life cycle is how a living thing changes during its life.

limestone, page 74.
Limestone is a kind of rock. It is much softer than granite.

links, page 60.
Links are the parts of a chain.

loam, page 80.
Loam is a dark soil with a mix of sand, silt, clay, and humus. It is a good soil for plants.

lodge, page 64.
A beaver's lodge is the home the beaver builds in the water, using branches from trees.

long bones, page 40.
The bones in your arms and legs are long bones.

luster, page 76.
Luster is the way a mineral looks when light hits it.

M

magma, page 118.
Magma is hot matter found inside Earth.

mammals, page 34.
A mammal is an animal whose life cycle includes a part when it nurses on its mother's milk. Squirrels, dogs, bears, and humans are mammals.

matter, page 92.
Matter is anything that takes up space. Rain, snow, oceans, air, and clouds in the sky are all examples of matter.

medicines, page 66.
Medicines help stop sickness and pain.

minerals, pages 50 and 74.
Along with vitamins, minerals help your body grow and stay healthy. Rocks are made from minerals.

muscles, page 44.
Muscles make bones move.

N

natural, page 74.
Natural things are not made by people.

natural gas, page 112.
Natural gas is a kind of fossil fuel.

natural resources, page 108.
Natural resources, such as stones and trees, are materials people use. These materials are found where people live.

nectar, page 12.
Nectar is a sweet juice made by some flowers.

nest, page 28.
Many birds build nests. They lay their eggs in the nest and use it as a home for the baby birds.

nursing, page 34.
Nursing is the second part of a mammal's life cycle. It is the time when it feeds on its mother's milk.

O

oil, page 112.
Oil is a kind of fossil fuel.

P

pistil, page 10.
The pistil is the female part of a flower.

pivot joints, page 42.
Pivot joints let bones turn and twist. Elbows are pivot joints.

plant-eaters, page 60.
Plant-eaters are animals that use plants for food.

pollen, page 10.
Pollen is made by a plant's stamen. Pollen joins with an egg, made by a plant's pistil, to form a seed.

pollination, page 10.
Pollination takes place when pollen from a plant's stamen sticks to a pistil.

pores, page 80.
Pores are the spaces between pieces of soil.

power plant, page 112.
A power plant makes electricity for a town or city. Some power plants use running water. Others use fossil fuels, such as oil, coal, and natural gas.

properties, page 74.
Properties are a thing's qualities—what color it is, how hard it is, how heavy it is, and so on.

pupa, page 30.
The pupa is the third part of a butterfly's life cycle. In this part, the larva, or caterpillar, makes a hard covering.

R

rain, page 96.
Rain is the part of the water cycle that you can see.

recycle, page 114.
To recycle things means to use old things to make new ones.

reduce, page 114.
To reduce using something, like electricity, means to use less of it.

reptile, page 32.
A reptile is an animal, like a turtle or a snake, that lays its eggs on dry land.

reuse, page 114.
To reuse things means to use them over again instead of throwing them away.

ribs, page 40.
Ribs are bones in your chest.

S

seeds, page 8.
Many plants grow from seeds. This is the beginning of the plant's life cycle.

shelter, page 108.
A shelter, such as a tent or house, keeps people dry in the rain. It keeps them warm in winter and cool in summer.

silt, page 80.
Silt is soil that feels soft and smooth.

skeleton, page 40.
A human skeleton is made of all the bones inside the body. It holds the body up.

skull, page 40.
Your skull is all the bones in your head.

sliding joints, page 42.
Sliding joints allow bones to turn and bend. They are found in the spine.

smog, page 100.
Smog is air pollution mixed with fog.

sodium, page 76.
The element sodium is a soft metal.

soil, page 78.
Soil is made of tiny pieces of rock and dead plants and animals.

solar energy, page 118.
Solar energy is energy from the sun. It can be turned into energy for our homes.

spine, page 40.
The small bones that run down the middle of your back are part of your spine.

stamen, page 10.
The stamen is the male part of a flower.

stratus clouds, page 98.
Stratus clouds look like flat, white sheets. They float near the ground.

T

tadpole, page 32.
The tadpole is the part of a frog's life cycle between the egg and the adult frog. The tadpole lives only in the water.

temperature, page 92.
Temperature is the level of heat energy in a piece of matter.

tendons, page 44.
Tendons are long, thin bands that tie muscles to bones.

texture, page 80.
Texture is how something feels when you touch it.

thermometer, page 92.
A thermometer measures the temperature of matter.

thistle, page 16.
A thistle is a plant whose seeds stick to animal fur and clothing.

V

vitamins, page 50.
Along with minerals, vitamins help your body grow and stay healthy.

W

walking stick, page 64.
A walking stick is an insect that looks like a tiny branch.

water cycle, page 96.
Water on Earth moves through the water cycle as it keeps changing form. Over and over again, the water evaporates, condenses, and falls as rain, snow, or ice.

water vapor, page 96.
Water vapor is the gas that liquid water changes into when it evaporates.

weather, page 90.
Weather is what the air is like outside. Weather changes all the time.

weathering, page 78.
Weathering is the wearing away of rocks by wind, rain, and ice.

weather vane, page 94.
A weather vane measures the direction from which wind is blowing.

wind, page 94.
Wind forms when cold air pushes warm air.

windmills, page 118.
Windmills have blades that turn in the wind. Windmills can change wind energy into electrical energy.

wires, page 112.
Wires are used to bring electricity from a power plant to your home. Wires that are in the walls of your house carry the electricity to the things that use it.